YOU LOSE SOME, YOU LOSE SOME

YOU LOSE SOME, YOU LOSE SOME

The beyond-belief
screwed-up seasons,
gruesome games,
doomed dynasties,
failed favorites,
pitiful players, and
fouled-up franchises
in the history of sports

by Eric Furman & Lou Harry

YOU LOSE SOME, YOU LOSE SOME

Copyright © 2004 by Eric Furman and Lou Harry
Library of Congress Cataloging-in-Publication Data
Furman, Eric, 1978– / Harry, Lou, 1963–
You Lose Some, You Lose Some / by Eric Furman and Lou Harry
p. cm. 1. Sports--United States--Anecdotes. 2. Losers--Anecdotes. I. II. Title.
GV583.F87 2004 796'.0973--dc22 2004018500 ISBN 1-57860-183-5
Cover photo by Grey Villet/Getty Images, Design by Evan Hale

Emmis Books
1700 Madison Road
Cincinnati, Ohio 45206
www.emmisbooks.com

TABLE OF CONTENTS

INTRODUCTION x

1 OLD-TIMERS' GAMES

1. 1916 Cumberland Bulldogs 16

2. 1919 Black Sox 20

3. 1940 Redskins 28

4. 1951 Dodgers...32

5. 1952 Muncie Central..42

2 DYNASTIES AREN'T FOREVER...THANK GOD

6. USA Little League Baseball 52

7. Minnesota Vikings 56

8. L.A. Clippers...63

9. Prairie View A&M Football..70

3 THE WHOLE WORLD IS WATCHING: THE OLYMPICS

10. Jim Thorpe 76

11. Adolf Hitler, 1936 Olympics 83

12. 1972 USA Silver Medal Basketball Team 87

13. Mary Decker..93

14. Tonya Harding 98

4 SEASONS ON THE STINK

15. 1962 New York Mets..104

16. 1972 Philadelphia 76ers...110

17. 1976 Tampa Bay Buccaneers 114

18. 1992-93 Ottawa Senators & San Jose Sharks 118

5 CHOKE HOLDERS

19. 1964 Philadelphia Phillies 126

20. 1969 Chicago Cubs 132

21. 1978 Boston Red Sox 137

22. Greg Norman 146

23. Chris Webber...150

24. Jean van de Velde 156

6 FREAK SHOWINGS

25. The Zamboni Game..162

26. Don Denkinger and the '85 Cardinals 166

27. Mike Tyson...174

28. Bobby Riggs..179

7 UNHAPPY ENDINGS

29. 1982 Stanford Football 186

30. Leon Durham..192

31. John Elway, Super Bowl XXIV 199

32. Scott Norwood 204

33. 1986 California Angels 210

34. Andres Escobar 217

35. Buckner 221

APPENDIX

A. All the Field's a Stage 225

B. Concrete Voices...228

C. Leagues of Their Own Doing 230

INTRODUCTION 1 by Lou Harry

I LOST TO Colts defensive lineman Dwight Freeney.

I lost to IndyCar driver Michael Andretti.

Then again, I kicked Colts' wide receiver Marvin Harrison's ass.

So, you see, I know both sides of this win/loss game. I know the thrill of victory and the agony of defeat.

More importantly, I know that it doesn't really matter who wins or loses. What matters is that there's a good story. One of these days, if we bump into each other, I'll tell you the story about Freeney. And the one about Andretti. And especially the Harrison saga.

In the meantime, you've got a bookload of tales to read that don't involve me. They involve a who's who of sports greats and sports unknowns, many of whom have had really, really off days. Our desire in chronicling these tales of woe is to entertain sports nuts and casual fans alike with the good and funny and sad and compelling stories behind some of the most humiliating defeats in sports history.

We hope you cringe...and enjoy.

INTRODUCTION 2 by Eric Furman

LET'S GET A few things straight, right off the bat: (1) Lou went head-to-head with Dwight Freeney in a video game. (2) If you push Lou hard enough, he'll admit that his loss to Michael Andretti was on a go-kart track. And (3) the game in which he "kicked Colts' wide receiver Marvin Harrison's ass" was bowling. Celebrity bowling.

Lou makes it sound a lot more glamorous than it really is, doesn't he?

There's an old saying, which I will here attribute to the film Braveheart: "History is written by those who've hanged heroes."

Translation: History is written by those who've won.

Winners get to do all the cool stuff: smoke cigars, pour champagne on each other's heads, write history, hang heroes…

But what about the losers?

"Why should we pay them any mind?" you ask. "They're losers. They don't deserve our attention."

Well, I don't mean to sound preachy here, but—No, you know what? Yes I do. See, I taught seventh and eighth graders for a year, and I saw a whole bunch of kids who were being sheltered from losing. They were allowed to retake failed tests until they passed, they weren't allowed to keep score in gym class, and there was no such thing as "cuts" on the various sports teams—everybody made it.

To be real honest, this made me want to punch somebody. Not the kids, of course, but the adults—wherever they might be—who implement these way-too-sheltering rules. What did they think they were going to do, eliminate losing from our society altogether?

Sorry, folks, but we're stuck with it. Because in order to have winners, you've got to have losers. And guess what? We're all losers. Each and every one of us. We've lost way more than we've won in our lifetimes. And we're in good company. Michael Jordan. Muhammad Ali. Donald Trump. Bill Clinton. All, at one time or another, losers.

Yet here we are, trying to keep our kids from feeling that stomach-tightening embarrassment and heartache that comes with losing.

Why would we do that?

Losing is not great. (Okay, it sucks.) But it is necessary. It is vital to our experience here on this sphere. The fact that we lose so much is what makes the winning so—for lack of a better word—special. We crave those moments when we feel like a real winner because they just don't happen all that much. And you know what? THAT'S OKAY! That's the way it's always been. Just ask Scott Norwood or Mary Decker or John Elway or Greg Norman or Bill Buckner or anybody else in this book. Hell, ask Lou. He's lost 67 percent of the time he's squared off against a professional athlete.

So...all you parents out there who are afraid of your kid losing (or, worse—failing): Let him know about Jean van de Velde. Tell her the story of Muncie Central. Let him read about Gene Mauch and the California Angels. (It'll work a lot like when you had your heart broken and you listened to "Everybody Hurts," by R.E.M., over and over again.)

And for all you kids out there (young and not-so-young alike), know this: You win some and you lose some. But mostly, you lose some.

1

OLD-TIMERS' GAMES

1

THE YEAR: 1916
THE VENUE: Georgia Tech's football stadium, Atlanta
THE EVENT: Georgia Tech Yellow Jackets vs. the Cumberland Bulldogs

JOHN HEISMAN was an impressive man. He had a law degree from the University of Pennsylvania. He was a noted public speaker. A part-time Shakespearean actor. A baseball coach.

Mostly, he was an outstanding football coach, perhaps the best in the nation. He had directed successful programs at Oberlin, Akron, Auburn and Clemson, and was now building a juggernaut at Georgia Tech. Heisman was known as an innovator, having invented the offensive formation shift, advocated the forward pass, and implemented the center toss (instead of the kick or roll) to the quarterback.

He was also known as a sore loser. A *very* sore loser.

Which was why, when Cumberland's *baseball* team whupped Heisman's Georgia Tech squad that past spring 22-0, they had to have known Coach H would get his day of revenge. That day would be October 7, on the gridiron instead of the baseball diamond.

Heisman's Georgia Tech team was a powerhouse. They were undefeated the previous season, and undefeated up to that point in 1916. The Yellow Jackets had thoroughly destroyed their opponents, outscoring them 294-24.

Cumberland, on the other hand, was a rag-tag group participating in a football program that could hardly be considered "on firm footing." In fact, the sport was dropped at Cumberland in 1906, resumed in 1912, and dropped again in 1915.

They had played a few games that year, including a 100-0 loss to Sewanee. But the team included only a few regular players and didn't even have a coach. Student-manager George Allen ran things, recruiting some of his Kappa Sigma brothers for game days when the team was short. Rag-tag, indeed.

But John Heisman couldn't stomach the spring's baseball loss to Cumberland. He'd convinced Georgia Tech's higher-ups to guarantee Cumberland $500 to come to Atlanta for this football game.

Five-hundred dollars was a weighty sum in those days, especially in the low-revenue world of amateur athletics. Cumberland couldn't turn down the money. If Heisman was willing to buy himself an overmatched opponent, the Bulldogs would be willing to be just that.

George Allen and fifteen other players boarded a Pullman train car in Lebanon, Tennessee, bound for Atlanta. But Allen must've known how awful his team was—after all, he stopped in Nashville to recruit players from Vanderbilt University. Frustratingly, he could find no takers. And what's worse, three of the Cumberland players remained in Nashville when the train left the station, leaving Allen's boys to field a squad of just thirteen. Nobody could've had a good feeling at that moment.

John Heisman—prior to the game—had decided that Tech would field two squads during the game, and they should play alternating quarters. To sweeten the deal, the coach even promised a steak dinner to the team that scored the most points.

After Cumberland's futile opening possession, Georgia Tech received the ball. Just under a minute into the contest, All-American Everett Strupper scored the first touchdown on a 20-yard run.

On offense, Cumberland found itself losing yards much more quickly than it gained them. The offense was so inept, and the game got so heinous, that two things happened before the end of the first quarter:

1. The Bulldogs began to punt the ball back to the Yellow Jackets immediately after Tech kicked off to them;

2. Heisman and Allen agreed to shorten the length of each period, from fifteen minutes to twelve-and-a-half.

Why? Because by the end of the first, Heisman's Team One had scored nine touchdowns. Cumberland had not even gained a positive yard. Tech's second team, playing the entire second period, also scored 63 points on nine touchdowns.

In the locker room at halftime, with a 126-0 lead, Heisman felt compelled to motivate his troops. "You're doing all right, team," he said. "We're ahead. But you just can't tell what those Cumberland players have up their sleeves. They may spring a surprise. Be alert, men! Hit 'em clean, but hit 'em hard!"

Needless to say, the score mounted. After the third period, Tech had 180 points, already surpassing Michigan's record of 153 points scored in a single collegiate football game. (Team One was *really* going for that steak dinner.) Everett Strupper was leading the charge with six touchdowns. He had a very clear path to the end zone for his seventh when, suddenly, he stopped at the 1-yard line. He leaned over and set the ball down on the grass. Canty Alexander—a beloved Tech teammate who had been trying to score unsuccessfully for three seasons now—picked up the purposeful fumble and dove into the end zone for his first collegiate touchdown.

The Cumberland thirteen were not amused.

They were also not amused a short time later, when one of their ball carriers fumbled the ball. As it rolled toward B.F. "Bird" Paty, the fumbler shouted, "Pick it up!" And Paty replied, "Pick it up yourself. You dropped it."

By the end of the embarrassing game, the Bulldogs had given up 222 points. They'd scored none. The offense's total net yardage was *minus 28*, and they had not garnered a single first down. Not one. (They did, however, gain 10 yards on a forward pass. Unfortunately, it was fourth-and-22 at the time.) The good news: Cumberland gave up zero first downs. The bad news: Georgia Tech scored within four downs every time they touched the ball, usually on first down.

Tech set so many records in this game, it's hard to keep track. But here are a few of the most stunning numbers:

Most points scored in a game by a single collegiate team (obviously).

Most rushing yards in a game by a single team (978).

Most points kicked after a touchdown by one player (18 by Jim Preas).

Most points scored in a quarter (63).

Most players scoring touchdowns (13).

In the aftermath, Morgan Blake of the *Atlanta Journal* wrote of the game: "With all due regard to the Tech team, it must be admitted that the tremendous score was due more to the pitifully weak opposition than to any unnatural strength on the part of the victors. In fact, as a general rule, the only thing necessary for a touchdown was to give Tech back the ball and holler, 'Here he comes' and 'There he goes.'

"The Lebanon boys were absolutely minus any apparent football virtues. They couldn't run with the ball, they couldn't block and they couldn't tackle. At spasmodic intervals they were able to down a runner, but they were decidedly too light and green to be effective at any stage of the game."

The Lebanon boys were, however, going home with $500. Sure, they would forever be known as the team who suffered the worst loss in the history of college football. But it could've been worse: They could have been on the winning side. Immediately after the game, John Heisman put his team through a brutal thirty minute scrimmage and told his squad it had played a "fairly good game."

But Heisman was not all mind games and unfair motivational ploys. He did decide that since his first team scored 117 points in their two quarters against Cumberland, and his second team scored 105 points, *everyone* would get that steak dinner.

2

THE REPORTERS were the first ones to sniff it out. Sitting in the press box in Cincinnati, awaiting the first pitch of the year's World Series between the hometown Reds and the heavily favored Chicago White Sox, Hugh Fullerton of the *Chicago Herald and Examiner* announced to his colleagues: "Every dog in the streets knows it smells. Keep your eyes open. A lot of strange things may happen before this series ends."

It was, in fact, a strange statement from Fullerton, one taken special note of by his journalistic fraternity brothers. Damon Runyon, Taylor Spink, Ring Lardner, and Westbrook Pegler—the most notable sports columnists of the day—had all known Fullerton to be the most accurate forecaster among them, and he had, until that time, been unhesitatingly predicting that the White Sox would easily win the World Series.

But suddenly, he made a proclamation that something stank in Mudville. And more: All-time baseball great Christy Mathewson—who had thrown three World Series shutouts in 1905 and was retired after a tour of duty in World War I—would be sitting next to Fullerton throughout the series, keeping tabs and circling in red questionable plays on a wirebound scorebook.

Why the suspicion? Fullerton and his colleagues needed look no further than the gamblers. They played a much larger role and were more connected to ballplayers than anyone wanted to admit. This was mainly due to the war: In 1917, the government ordered all horse racing suspended until war's end. Baseball, however, was allowed to continue. So gamblers took a strong interest in the national pastime. The lobbies of hotels where major league teams stayed had become congregating areas for dirty money men; the baseball diamond was where the action could be found.

Just a few days earlier, the White Sox were a 3-1 betting favorite to win the series. Everyone agreed those odds were on target. The American League—to which the Sox belonged—had won eight of the last nine series. This year, the White Sox had been, hands down, baseball's best team, with an overall batting average of .287 and a league-leading 668 runs scored. Plus, position by position, to a man, the White Sox had a stronger team than the Reds.

At catcher: fiery Ray Schalk, a future Hall of Famer who revolutionized his position. (He was the first to run down the first- and third-base lines to provide backup in case of a wild throw.)

Chick Gandil was a slick first baseman, a big, muscular man (6 feet 2 inches, 200 pounds), and a steady hitter.

Second baseman Eddie Collins might just be the best second-sacker ever. He could bunt, slash, or hit and run. With an Ivy League education, he had been called, "the smartest man that ever walked on a ball field." And his intelligence and poise enabled him to make impossible plays.

Shortstop Swede Risberg was smooth enough in the field and had a powerful enough arm to allow Buck Weaver to return to his natural position, third base, for the 1919 season.

Weaver was a switch-hitter, but his defense was his strongest suit; he was the only man Ty Cobb would not bunt against.

Center fielder Happy Felsch, who led the league in assists that year, attracted attention for his range in the outfield and for his cannon of a throwing arm. Shano Collins, in his ninth season with the Sox, capably manned right field.

And then there was "Shoeless" Joe Jackson. The left fielder had hit over .370 three times in his career up to that point. His batting average for the 1910s was .354 and his slugging average was over .500. (In fact, his .356 lifetime batting average left him *third* on the all-time list.) Jackson was swift in the outfield and threw with incredible accuracy. His swing was naturally flawless, the envy of the best hitters in the game. Ty Cobb said, "Joe Jackson hit the ball harder than any man ever to play the game. What's more, he would have gone down as the greatest batter of all time had he made a study of the scientific side of the batting art."

The Chicago pitching staff was just as strong as its everyday players. Eddie Cicotte was a deceptive hurler, with pinpoint control and the ability to change speeds. He led the league that season in wins (29), innings pitched (307) and complete games (30). Lefty Williams started a league-high forty games, and won twenty-three. And rookie Dickie Kerr won thirteen games to round out the first-rate staff.

Clearly, Charles Comiskey had assembled the best team in baseball, maybe its best ever. Equally clear is why 3-1 odds on them winning the World Series were probably not low enough.

If ever there was a sure thing, this was it. This best-of-nine series could be a five-game sweep. But then...

The gamblers' books suddenly did a 180-degree turn. All kinds of money began to quickly appear, all of it laid down by bettors who favored the Reds. This was not just a few folks hoping to cash in on a wild underdog pick. This was the kind of money a stockbroker with inside information would lay down.

Hugh Fullerton was on the scent, and the rest of his journalistic pals—including Christy Mathewson—were searching for the rotten signs of scandal. As John Philip Sousa stepped up on the band podium to conduct the national anthem at the start of Game 1, the press corps was on high alert. This was what they saw:

Game 1: Cicotte's first pitch was a fastball. A strike. His second hit Cincinnati leadoff man Maurice Rath right in the middle of his back.

Christy Mathewson drew the first red circle in his scorebook, less than a minute into the series. A bad sign.

In the bottom of the fourth inning, with the score tied 1-1, Reds pitcher Dutch Ruether stepped to the plate with two runners already on base.

Pitchers were weak hitters to begin with, and Ruether was on the lousy end of the scale. But he hit Cicotte's second pitch to the fence in center field. Both runners scored, and Ruether ended up with a triple.

Red circle number two.

But that wasn't the worst of it. The next two batters tattooed Cicotte's pitches into the outfield, and two more runs scored. Five straight hits. Five runs scored. And Cicotte hadn't allowed anything like that all year.

White Sox manager Kid Gleason angrily yanked him from the game.

In the locker room after the 9-1 drubbing, the White Sox were a silent group. Except one. Catcher Ray Schalk was highly animated, wondering to anybody who'd listen why Cicotte kept crossing him up on his signals. He said Cicotte repeatedly threw fastballs when he called for spitters, spitters when he called for fastballs, and change-ups in the most inopportune spots.

Newsman Hugh Fullerton walked through the locker room, telling people: "I don't like what I saw out there today. There is something smelly. Cicotte doesn't usually pitch like that."

Game 2: As Cincinnatians woke up on October 2, they found that the Reds were now favored by oddsmakers at 7-10. As game time neared, Kid Gleason told Schalk to keep a close eye on Sox pitcher Lefty Williams. But Williams breezed through the first three innings.

It was the fourth inning that proved to be his undoing. He walked one man. Then another. He gave up a single. And after Schalk gunned down a would-be base-stealer at second, Williams walked his third batter of the inning. Considering he had walked only fifty-eight men in 297 innings pitched over the course of the year, Sox fans know this was something more than out-of-the-ordinary for Williams. Christy Mathewson, Hugh Fullerton, and Ring Lardner knew it, too.

By the time Cincy's shortstop tripled in two runs, the Reds had a firm grip on the outcome of the game. They won, 4-2, and Schalk was even more furious in the post-game locker room than the previous day. "Three fucking times, three times," he shouted at Gleason, "Williams shook off my signals for curveballs."

Game 3: The series shifted to Chicago, and Shoeless Joe Jackson continued right where he left off. After three hits in the last game, he roped a single into left field to start the second inning. Happy Felsch sacrificed him to second, and they both advanced on a wild, hurried throw by the Reds pitcher. Chick Gandil, Sox first baseman, came to the plate and half-heartedly took a swing at the first pitch he saw. He hit a chopper through the drawn-in infield—almost looked accidental—and drove both Jackson and Felsch home. Dickie Kerr, the babyface on the Sox staff, pitched a masterful complete game, allowing only three hits and shutting out the Reds. Maybe, the theory went, the White Sox weren't in on a fix, after all.

Or maybe they were only paid to throw the first couple of games.

Game 4: Cicotte was due to pitch again, and Kid Gleason seemed to be doubting him. Cicotte begged Gleason for a chance to vindicate himself for his effort in Game 1. Unfortunately, there would be no vindication this day. The pivotal error in the game was again Cicotte's. After he awkwardly fielded an infield tapper, he made a horrendous throw over the first baseman's head and into the outfield. The Reds runner ended up on second base. The next hitter, Larry Kopf, hit the ball into left field. Shoeless Joe uncorked a tremendous throw to home plate in an attempt to cut down the runner trying to score. Cicotte, standing to the left of the mound, stabbed at the ball as it passed over his head, and deflected it away from home plate. Most observers believed Jackson's throw would have nailed Duncan had Cicotte not tampered with it.

It was a red-circle play for sure—perhaps the series' most blatant—and it signaled that this White Sox team that had always found ways to win was now going out of its way to lose.

Game 5: Lefty Williams and Hod Eller, a specialist in trick deliveries, were engaged in a double shutout through five innings. It was a dramatic, tight pitchers' duel. But the sixth inning brought the rain for the Sox. Cincinnati's Edd Roush hit a blast toward Happy Felsch. The usually sure-handed center fielder, while on the run, appeared to lose the ball for a moment, then caught up with it again. He made an awkward two-handed lunge in an attempt to make the catch, but the ball popped out of his mitt. He scurried around trying to pick up the ball, and when he finally did, Felsch unleashed a powerful throw to the catcher, Schalk. Edd Roush and the ball arrived at the same time, and the umpire called the runner safe on a bang-bang play. All of Schalk's frustrations seemed to come pouring out as he screamed and cursed at umpire Cy Rigler. The Reds scored three more runs and won Game 5 by a score of 5-0.

Game 6: After four innings, the White Sox—with the best offense in baseball—had now gone twenty-six innings without scoring. They had scored only six runs through five games. Even Shoeless Joe, who had hit sporadically throughout the series, found himself in a slump, with three popups and a groundout in Game 5. But suddenly, startlingly, their bats came alive in the fifth inning. They scored four runs to tie the game up, and in the top of the tenth inning the Sox won on an RBI single by Chick Gandil. The Sox were one game from defeat, but a 4-2 deficit is not insurmountable.

Game 7: Cicotte finally showed up to pitch his game. He gave up only seven hits and one run, and the White Sox won, 4-1. Shoeless Joe Jackson collected two hits and two RBIs, and the Chicagoans' hope was renewed as their team seemed to be back on track.

Game 8: Fullerton and the rest of the press box caught on to the hope restored in White Sox nation. The writers were starting to believe that this great team may still have enough talent to overcome its earlier shoddy play and win the World Series. For Hugh Fullerton, it would restore his faith in the purity of the game of baseball. But a single, solitary gambler put a bullet right into Fullerton's faith. The gambler told him: "All the betting's on Cincinnati. It's going to be the biggest first inning you ever saw."

Lefty Williams walked the leadoff batter. Then Cincinnati's two-, three-, and four-hole hitters singled. The number five man doubled, and after just fourteen pitches, Kid Gleason pulled Williams out of the game.

By the eighth inning, Cincinnati led, 10-1. And that was all she wrote.

The Reds were World Champions. The White Sox were a shameful disgrace.

Fullerton, in his column the day after the series ended, wrote:

There will be a great deal written about the World Series. There will be a lot of inside stuff that never will be printed. The truth will remain that the team which was the hardest working...won. The team which had the individual ability was beaten. They spilled the dope terribly...So much so that an evil-minded person might believe the stories that have been circulated during the Series. The fact is, this Series was lost in the first game.

Yesterday's, in all probability, is the last game that will ever be played in any World Series. If the club owners and those who have the interest of the game at heart have listened during the Series, they will call off the annual inter-league contest...Yesterday's game also means the disruption of the Chicago White Sox ball club. There are seven men on the team who will not be there when the gong sounds next spring.

Fullerton would be right about so many things. The 1919 World Series was lost in the first game, as soon as Cicotte plunked Maurice Rath between the shoulder blades with his second pitch. These would not be the last World Series games ever played, but baseball would do its best to ensure that no such scandal would ever rock its highest-profile event again. Eight White Sox players were subpoenaed to testify in front of a grand jury of Cook County, Illinois. They admitted to a conspiracy to throw games, from which they received only a small portion of the money gamblers had promised them.

The owners banded together and elected Judge Kenesaw Mountain Landis the new commissioner of baseball. Judge Landis would have "the authority to do anything I consider right in any matter detrimental to baseball...Neither faults in the law, miscarriages in the courts, or complaisance of magnates will prevent me from taking action in every case where I feel there was wrongdoing."

And with this supreme, unconditional authority—bestowed by the owners in their effort to clean up their cash-cow game—Landis promptly threw eight White Sox players out of baseball. For life.

They would be branded "losers" by their beloved game. They would be branded the "Black Sox" by the media. And they would be branded "traitors" by the fans who adored them.

Fullerton famously wrote that, as Shoeless Joe Jackson was escorted from the courthouse in which he testified on the matter of throwing the 1919 World Series, a young kid pressed forward and said, "Say it ain't so, Joe."

And Joe Jackson himself would refute that story, just like he refuted his guilt in the conspiracy to throw games: "No such word 'Say it ain't so' was ever said. The fellow who wrote that just wanted something to say. When I came out of the courthouse that day, nobody said anything to me. The only guy who spoke was a guy who yelled at his friend, 'I told you the big son of a bitch wore shoes.' I walked right out of there and stepped into my car and drove off."

THE YEAR: 1940
THE VENUE: Washington, D.C.'s Griffith Stadium
THE EVENT: The NFL title game between the Washington Redskins and the Chicago Bears

"CONGRATULATIONS. I hope I will have the pleasure of beating your ears off next Sunday and every year to come. We should play for the championship every year." These were the words of the telegram sent from Redskins owner George Preston Marshall to the Chicago Bears on the eve of the teams' NFL Championship matchup in 1940.

Apparently, Mr. Marshall was a bit of a trash-talker.

And why not? His 'Skins had the NFL's best record at 9-2. They had a modern, high-powered passing attack, led by Slingin' Sammy Baugh—the naturally innovative quarterback from Texas Christian University. They had a great wingback in Jimmy Johnston, who led the team in receiving and rushes. They had a defense that was holding opponents to just 12 points per game.

Most importantly, as the NFL title game approached, Marshall's gang had whipped the Bears only three weeks earlier. They held George "Papa Bear" Halas' squad to a single, sorry field goal and pulled out the 7-3 victory on a controversial touchdown pass.

The Bears, of course, complained about the game-winning score to anyone who would listen—referees, newspapermen, the league office, their wives. This only made Marshall retaliate by calling the Bears a bunch of "crybabies" to a *Washington Post* reporter. Think that ended up in the next day's headlines? It sure did, and in the ensuing article, Marshall went on to say, "[The Bears] are a first-half club. They are quitters. They are the world's greatest crybabies."

Needless to say, Halas didn't take too kindly to Marshall's comments. In fact, his words only stoked the fire that already was the Redskins-Bears rivalry. See, Washington had defeated Chi-town by a 28-21 margin in 1937 to capture the league title. The following year, the Bears enacted their revenge in the regular season, 31-7. Then came the 7-3 controversy in the 1940 regular season. So when Halas saw the front page of the paper, he tore it off and posted it prominently in the Chicago dressing room. Motivation, he figured.

Marshall followed up his insult in the papers with the injury via telegram, including that bit about "having the pleasure of beating your ears off..."

As a result, not only were the Bears focused and well-prepared...they were incensed.

But let's focus on the preparation for a moment. Even as Sammy Baugh and the 'Skins were popularizing the modern, single-wing passing attack, the Bears were experimenting with the old-school, stodgy T-wing formation that had gone out of style with flappers and the Charleston.

Halas' idea—which was fleshed out by former University of Chicago coach Clark Shaughnessy—was to reinvigorate the T-formation with new wrinkles like men-in-motion, splits in the line, and flankers. Problem was, his team was having a hard time grasping these new concepts. They had moments of fluidity during that 1940 campaign—including 47 points scored on the Cleveland Rams, 37 on the New York football Giants, and 41 on the Green Bay Packers—but, for the most part, the Bears needed some help getting focused with the new offense.

Enter, George Preston Marshall.

Nothing makes a group of competitive athletes focus more than being trash-talked. And by trash-talked, we mean "disrespected." And by disrespected, we mean "the Bears are a bunch of crybabies."

By kickoff, the Bears weren't crying so much as they were stewing. With rage. But in a calm and focused way. (Think Inigo Montoya in *The Princess Bride*.)

Fifty-six seconds.

That's how long it took the Bears' T-wing offense to score. Bill Osmanski, with the help of a George Wilson bone-crushing block, swept around the left end and scampered 68 yards downfield for a touchdown.

Washington was stunned, but not wounded. At least, not yet.

They drove down into Chicago territory, and from the 26-yard line, Baugh tossed a perfect pass into the end zone. Charley Malone—as sure-handed a receiver as the Redskins had—was wide-open...waiting, waiting, waiting...and he dropped it.

From there, the Bears pounced. Three more touchdowns in the first half—the first on a Sid Luckman QB sneak, the second on a Joe Maniaci 42-yard sweep, and the third on a 30-yard pass from Luckman to Ken Kavanaugh—brought the score to 28-0 at the intermission.

The game was teetering on the verge of a blowout, and at this point, you'd think the Bears would slow things down, control the clock, and take home the championship.

But the Monsters of the Midway needed only to look up at the bulletin board in their locker room to be reminded of Mr. Marshall's barbs.

Back to work they went.

On the second play of the second half, Sammy Baugh, deep in his own territory, lofted a floater up in the air. Chicago's Hamp Pool intercepted it and returned it for another touchdown—35-0, Bears. A few minutes later, Baugh's fourth-and-20 attempt failed. The Bears took over on downs, and soon enough Ray Nolting was charging through a huge hole in the line and toward the end zone. Forty-one-zip. A minute later, another interception thrown by Baugh and it was 48-0. Before the third quarter was over, Baugh threw his *third* interception returned for a touchdown, and his 'Skins trailed, 54-0.

At the start of the fourth quarter, a frustrated Redskin punched a helmetless Bear in the face—good for a 15-yard penalty. The infraction also set up a quarterback reverse, and Harry Clark took the trick play all the way to give the Bears 60 points. A fumble recovery and a 2-yard dive brought the score to 66-0, and that's where the referees had to step in.

Because there were no nets behind the goal posts back then, Chicago had kicked eight balls into the stands—one for an extra point after each one of their touchdowns. Now this was a problem because the refs had only brought along nine. So head official William Friesell asked Halas not to kick for this one; to pass or run for it instead. The Bears went with the pass, the Redskins couldn't stop them (why start then?), and the score was 67-0.

After one more TD and failed extra-point conversion—on the heels of a sustained ten-play drive—the final tally was 73-0. Never mind championship game stats; this was the highest point total *and* greatest margin of victory in *any* NFL game *ever*.

The Bears only passed the ball eight times all day, but they racked up 372 yards on the ground and held the 'Skins to 3 yards rushing. Chicago also intercepted Slingin' Sammy Baugh eight times on the day, and five set up touchdowns.

Perhaps the most satisfying moment came when George Marshall turned on his own players late in the second half and screamed at them, calling *them* quitters. Oh, irony of ironies...

So you've got to wonder, how could two teams so evenly matched just three weeks earlier play a game that turned into this?

How could the Redskins hold the Chicago offense to only 3 points one time, then give up 73 the next?

How could a league championship game—pitting the two best teams the NFL had to offer—end up so lopsided?

The answer has to be momentum. The Bears had it from the beginning, when Marshall gave them something to play for. They kept it rolling with each successive interception or long run from the T-formation.

And the Redskins could never get it, especially once the Bears struck first. Sure, Washington had its chance, but then wide-open Charley Malone dropped Baugh's touchdown pass, and that was all she wrote.

In the aftermath of the destruction, a reporter asked Baugh if things might have gone different had Malone not dropped the sure touchdown pass.

"Yep," Baugh said. "It would have been 73-7."

4

ANY SPORTS FAN worth his salt has seen the grainy TV footage or spied a black-and-white photo of perhaps the most indelible baseball moment of all time: Bobby Thomson's "Shot Heard 'Round the World."

And if he hasn't seen it, he's heard play-by-play man Russ Hodges' unbridled ecstasy: "The Giants win the pennant! The Giants win the pennant! The Giants win the pennant! The Giants win the pennant! Bobby Thomson hits it into the lower deck of the left-field stands! The Giants win the pennant and they're going crazy, they're going crazy. Ooooohhhheeee."

It's a moment that captures in one still-frame the neck-hair-raising-est thrill sports can provide.

But that still-frame and that sound bite are only the culmination of a fantastically intriguing story. It's a story that tends to get left behind by those who tell history from a Cliffs Notes perspective. It's a story that began as the 1951 season got out of the gate with the Brooklyn Dodgers tearing out of the starting position and the New York Giants falling flat on their faces.

The Dodgers were loaded with talent. Just check out these names. A lightning-fast, tough-as-nails cleanup hitter named Jackie Robinson. A catcher, and league MVP in '51, named Roy Campanella. A sure-handed shortstop named Pee Wee Reese. A smooth-fielding slugger at first base named Gil Hodges. A lefthanded-hitting center fielder named Duke Snider. A cannon-armed right fielder named Carl Furillo. And a pitching staff with the likes of Don Newcombe, Preacher Roe, Carl Erskine, and Ralph Branca.

When these Dodgers added All-Star left fielder Andy Pafko on June 16—to shore up the only hole in their already-dominant squad—a pennant seemed assured.

The Giants were certainly no threat. Beginning the season losing twelve of their first fourteen ballgames, they seemed headed for certain disaster by mid-May. Sad, because Leo Durocher—one of the great characters of the game—left the Dodgers in 1948 to manage the crosstown Giants.

It was a controversial move, but Leo "The Lip" had worn out his welcome with Dodger ownership. With the Giants, his task was to put together a team. Three years later, before the season started, he finally believed he had the right ingredients. Monte Irvin, blossoming as a powerful, clutch-hitting first baseman. Don Mueller, a strongman right fielder who made a bat look like a toothpick in his hands. Bobby Thomson, a steady, All-Star-caliber center fielder. Alvin Dark and Eddie Stanky, a winning double-play combo in the middle infield. Sal Maglie, an ace that nobody knew the Giants had, coming off a dominant 18-4 record in 1950.

These Giants were a competitive group that finished in third place in the 1950 season, only five games behind the Philadelphia Phillies.

Expectations were high for '51—which is why their 2-12 start was an absolute mystery: Something was severely off in Durocher's recipe.

Enter: Willie Howard Mays, Jr., aka "The Say Hey Kid." (He had a hard time remembering names, so his usual direct address was, "Hey.") Mays, a twenty-year-old rookie who got his first shot at the bigs on May 25, had a rough start, going hitless in his first twelve at-bats during a weekend series with the Phillies. But he soon showed his potential in his first appearance at the Polo Grounds. Facing future Hall of Famer Warren Spahn, Mays smashed a home run onto the left field roof.

It was just the spark the Giants needed.

Everyone—including Durocher and Thomson—could see he was gifted enough to become one of the greatest players to occupy center field. He covered the grass like a tent and threw baseballs like he was shooting

BBs. This much was plain to see: Mays was going to force center fielder Thomson to move elsewhere. After a short stint in left, Durocher tried him as a third baseman. Here Thomson seemed to shine. He enjoyed being on top of every pitch, chatting up the hitters, and preparing for a hot smash to come his way. On July 20, as a newly installed third sacker, Bobby Thomson had a new lease on what had heretofore been the most disappointing season he could remember.

Still, there were the crosstown Dodgers to contend with. On August 9, the Dodgers completed a three-game sweep of the Giants at Ebbets Field in Brooklyn. The three victories gave the Dodgers a seemingly insurmountable twelve-game lead in the standings—and the winners had no qualms about gloating.

There used to be a wooden door between the Dodgers' clubhouse and the visitors' clubhouse at Ebbets Field. The door was always locked and bolted, but it was also thin enough to hear through. As the two teams dressed after the game on August 9, the Giants could hear singing coming from the other side of that wooden door.

"Roll out the barrel/We got the Giants on the run..."

Dodger manager Charlie Dressen had organized the chorus. Some of the players, like pitcher Ralph Branca, thought it was a bad idea that could only lead to trouble. But that didn't stop those taunters who joined in. Nor did it stop Jackie Robinson, who was slamming a bat against the wooden door and yelling, "Eat your heart out, Leo."

Giant Eddie Stanky got angry.

"Shove that bat up your ass," he shouted.

The rest of the Giants waited for Durocher to react with the same degree of anger. But the coach kept dressing and said quietly: "I don't have to make any speeches. If that doesn't wake you up, nothing will."

Two days later, in between games of a doubleheader with the Braves, the Dodgers enjoyed their largest lead of the season: 13½ games. And there were only 48 remaining.

By the time September rolled around, the Dodgers were putting up stats that could have given their statistician carpal tunnel syndrome. Roy

Campanella was batting .316 with 28 homers and 89 RBIs; Gil Hodges had 36 homers and 88 runs batted in; Duke Snider had 28 homers and 92 RBIs; and Jackie Robinson was leading the team with a .342 batting average, and had 16 homers and 73 runs batted in.

The pitching staff was just as sparkling: Roe's won-loss record was 18-2; Newcombe, 17-7; Erskine, 14-9; Branca, 13-9; and Clyde King, 14-6.

King was a reliever, for crying out loud.

The Dodgers were more than numbers, though. They were a proud, uber-confident team, that liked to grandstand and taunt (see clubhouse singing, above), but who couldn't stand it when somebody else returned the favor.

Example: On September 2, Giant right fielder Don Mueller was heading to bat having already hit four home runs in two weekend games against Brooklyn. Before coming to bat, a teammate informed him that his wife had given birth to his first son. Crash. There went home run number five. As Mueller rounded third, he shouted to Durocher, "It's a boy! It's a boy!"

Surely anyone could understand his joy.

Not Dodger pitcher Phil Haugstad, who seemed to think Mueller was showing him up. He reacted to Mueller's jolly jaunt around the bases by drilling the Giants' next two hitters, Thomson and Mays.

"One more like that," warned plate umpire Al Barlick, "and you're gone, *too*."

He would have been in good company. Earlier in the game, Barlick had already ejected Branca and Dick Williams from the Dodgers' dugout. Newcombe was tossed in the sixth for arguing balls and strikes. And he also thumbed Jackie Robinson and pitcher Clem Labine. In reaction to all the ejections, Dressen cleared his bench with a whistle and a finger-point. Sent the whole team into the clubhouse, where he knew they wouldn't be able to be ejected.

Dressen also knew he was being a real smartass. Haugstad didn't get ejected, but Dressen's attitude and defiant display showed that, apparently, the clubhouse singing wasn't an isolated incident.

Further proof that the Dodgers walked the fine line came when Don Newcombe asked Dodgers G.M. Buzzie Bavasi for $5,000.

"What for?" Bavasi asked.

"I want to buy a Cadillac," Newcombe said.

"You don't need $5,000."

"I do for the one I want," Newcombe said. "It's a Cadillac Sedan de Ville, sky blue. My first Cadillac."

"When do I get it back?" asked Bavasi.

"Keep my Series share," Newcombe replied.

There were still twenty-one games left in the season when Newcombe asked for the advance against his World Series pay.

Plenty of time for his team to earn a place in this book.

But time *was* running out for the Giants. With only thirteen games left in the season, the Dodgers were still ahead by eight. They began to talk openly to the press about their possible World Series opponents. (The Yankees trailed the Cleveland Indians by one-half game in the American League.) "The Yankees would be tougher than Cleveland," said Jackie Robinson. "The Yankees have a way of rising to the occasion."

When Campanella was beaned in the head two games later, and the beat writers questioned Dressen about his catcher's health, he said, "Campy's still woozy. No reason to play him now. I want him ready for the World Series."

Two nights after that, before a home game against the Braves, Dressen was celebrated on his home field, in front of his adoring Brooklyn fans. He stood at home plate and accepted a $5,000 savings bond, a cream-colored Dodge station wagon, a floral horseshoe, and an oil portrait identifying him as the manager of the "National League Champions, *1951*."

That may have been the kiss of death.

In the next few days, the Dodgers three-game lead would slip down to one.

And still they cared little about angering the baseball gods.

In the eighth inning of an all-important blowout victory over the Braves, Jackie Robinson stole home on rookie righthander Lew Burdette. The play gave the Dodgers a 14-3 lead. And it gave the Braves something to play for the next day.

"Stealing home in that situation is bush baseball," one of the Braves said as the two teams crossed paths on the way to their respective clubhouses. "We'll get you bastards tomorrow."

They sure got 'em. In a hotly contested game, a bang-bang play at the plate gave the Braves a 4-3 lead. Campanella had the plate blocked, but umpire Frank Dascoli signaled the Braves runner safe. Campanella couldn't take the frustration or the pressure. He slammed his glove into the dirt. Dascoli quickly gave him the thumb. In a wild scene, longtime coach Cookie Lavagetto was also ejected—his only boot in all his years in baseball.

The Campanella ejection really cost the Dodgers the game. He would have had a chance to bat in the ninth inning with a runner on third—a situation where a fly ball would have been enough. But instead Wayne Terwilliger, a .227-hitting utility infielder, hit a light chopper to the third baseman, who held the runner and nailed Terwilliger at first. Pafko struck out to end it, and suddenly the Dodgers were clinging to a half-game lead.

In the postgame madness, Campanella, Robinson, Roe and a few others waited for Dascoli at the door to the umpires' room. During a great commotion, Campy's shrill, animated voice could be heard questioning Dascoli. Suddenly, the panels on the umpires' door splintered and a security guard called for reinforcements. Six Boston policemen showed up on a scene wrought with frustration, anger, and pressure.

The Giants heard all about it. And as usual, Leo the Lip had plenty to say.

"I don't think [the Dodgers] can do it. They're screaming at umpires. Pretty soon they'll be screaming at each other. Pennant pressure can give the steadiest of pros the yips," Durocher said.

The pressure did get to the Dodgers. Going into the last day of the season, the two teams were tied in the standings.

With all the emotional grandeur that Bobby Thomson's home run brings to mind, it casts a long shadow over one of the greatest games ever played under pressure: the final regular-season game of that 1951 season, between the Brooklyn Dodgers and the Philadelphia Phillies.

The New York Giants had already won their game. And the Dodgers, on the field in their own contest, knew it. They dug themselves a 6-1 hole early, and when the Giants victory score was placed on the board in Philly's Shibe Park, the Brooklyn Bums were still down, 8-5. They knew that if they didn't pull out a win here, they were going home for the winter, losers of a thirteen-and-a-half-game lead.

Unfortunately, three runs down with three innings to go isn't the most optimistic position to be in. Still, the Dodgers rallied to tie the score at 8 in the eighth inning. This was new life.

And this was when Don Newcombe entered the game to pitch.

It was an incredible thing, because Newcombe had gone the distance the night before on just two days' rest. Now he was on the mound for do-or-die innings on only 16 *hours'* rest. He stayed in for five innings. But in the twelfth frame, Newcombe's arm finally began to wear down. He allowed the bases to be loaded with only one out. Then he reached down deep and got a tremendously clutch strikeout.

That's when the game turned into the Jackie Robinson show.

With two down and the bases still loaded, a weak-hitting reserve named Eddie Waitkus approached the plate, trying to end the Dodgers' season right there. He swung at his pitch, hit a sharp line-drive on a trajectory that would take it between Jackie Robinson and second base. He waited with the rest of the crowd to see what became of it.

Robinson dove. He stabbed at the ball backhanded. And when he skidded across the infield face-first, he also knifed his elbow into his solar plexus.

As he came to a halt, he flipped the white ball up to Reese and collapsed.

Robinson had knocked the wind out of himself, but he had also made one of the greatest game-saving (no, season-saving...no, hope-saving) catches of all time.

In the fourteenth, Robinson came to the plate. He later admitted he was "shooting for the stands," and that's exactly what he hit: the upper deck in left field.

It was a great moment—for Brooklyn, for the Dodgers, for Dressen, and mostly for Robinson. "Greatest home run I ever hit," he said after the game.

The joy turned quickly into relief, which turned quickly into reality: the Giants were waiting to start a three-game playoff series the next day at Ebbets Field.

• • •

It's common knowledge that the teams split the first two games, which forced a third game at the Polo Grounds. It's also common knowledge how that game ended—with Bobby Thomson's low liner ripped into the left-field bleachers.

But here's what happened in between: Bobby Thomson lashed a low line drive down the left-field line in the second inning. It was hit so hard that Thomson—who put his head down as he bore down on second base—didn't realize that Pafko had already fielded the ball and thrown it back to the infield. By the time Thomson caught on, he tried to turn back to first, but Hodges tagged him out. *Oh well*, he thought, *I'll get a chance to redeem myself.*

Don Newcombe mowed down Giants for six innings, running a shut-out streak to 20⅔ innings over three pressure-packed games. When the Giants held a mini-rally in the seventh and Monte Irvin ended up on third base with only one out, the Dodgers tried to pull the old hidden ball trick. But Giant Whitey Lockman—standing on first base—detected that third baseman Billy Cox was walking toward his position with the ball after a quick mound conference with Newcombe. The hidden ball trick was foiled, and Bobby Thomson tied the game with a long sacrifice fly to score Irvin.

Sal Maglie—the Giants' season-long ace—lost his verve in the eighth inning. He gave up three runs and handed the Dodgers the key to the World Series.

In the bottom of the ninth, Alvin Dark led things off with a squeaky single that dribbled just past the outstretched glove of Jackie Robinson. With Dark on first, Dressen elected to play Gil Hodges on the bag at first. This was a critical mistake, because Don Mueller laced a line drive into the hole that was previously occupied by Hodges. Dark scampered to third.

Monte Irvin came to the plate. He led the NL with 121 runs batted in, he considered himself a clutch hitter, and he thrived on pressure situations. But Irvin tried too hard this time and popped a foul ball harmlessly into the glove of Hodges near first base. It was a huge out, and it deflated the Polo Grounds crowd.

As Irvin hung his head on his way back to the dugout, the press box made a booming announcement: "Attention, press. World Series credentials for *Ebbets* Field can be picked up at six o'clock tonight at the Biltmore Hotel."

Uh-oh. Can you see the baseball gods messing with *everyone* after that?

Whitey Lockman stepped into the batter's box to face Newcombe. He wasn't there long. He whipped the first pitch into the leftfield corner for a standup double and a 4-2 ballgame. And Bobby Thomson was due up next.

But the game stopped. Don Mueller had stumbled into third base on Lockman's double. He twisted his right ankle, and x-rays would later show torn tendons. As the Giants' trainer examined the collapsed Mueller, Charlie Dressen made his way out to the mound for a conference. "What do you want to do?" he asked his infield, gathered with him on the mound. "It's your money as well as mine."

The Dodgers stood silent, shocked that this cocky, competitive, proud man—who usually had all the answers—was leaving a decision that could decide the pennant up to them.

Pee Wee Reese, the man they called "Captain," spoke up. "Newk's given us all he's got for the last week. Why don't you get somebody fresh in here."

And that was it. Fate was sealed.

Ralph Branca came in from the bullpen, where he had been warming up since the fifth inning. At the mound, he took the ball from Newcombe, smiled and said, "Don't worry about it, big fella. I'll take care of everything."

Branca knew how to pitch to Thomson. He remembered that two days before, in the playoff opener, Thomson had hit a homer on a fastball. This time, Branca wanted him to swing at a curve. But to get Thomson to bite, Branca would have to set him up with some heat. He threw one fastball, and Thomson took it. For his next pitch, Branca planned on wasting one up and inside, so that when he threw the curve down and away, Thomson wouldn't know what to expect.

Branca didn't get a chance to throw that curveball. He only got one more pitch...

"The Giants win the pennant! The Giants win the pennant! The Giants win the pennant! The Giants win the pennant! Bobby Thomson hits it into the lower deck of the left-field stands! The Giants win the pennant and they're going crazy, they're going crazy. Ooooohhhheeee."

As the Dodgers trickled into the clubhouse, with the city of New York celebrating above them, each player knew what had been lost. Along with the game and the season and the chance for glory, there was that most simple, essential thing that had been ripped out from their insides: pride.

All the assumptions and the brash words and the presumptive behavior could be balled up and thrown into the corner of a locker. Just like Jackie Robinson had done with his glove. Gil Hodges quietly had folded his own mitt and placed it on the top shelf of his locker. Charlie Dressen had exasperatedly ripped his uniform shirt off, buttons spraying everywhere.

But Ralph Branca, poor Ralph Branca...he crumpled onto the wooden steps of the two-level clubhouse. He drooped his head and hunched his shoulders, and you could barely make out his muttering: "Why me? Why me?"

5

THE YEAR: 1954
THE VENUE: Indianapolis' Butler Fieldhouse
THE EVENT: The state championship game, Milan Indians vs.
Muncie Central Bearcats

THOSE WHO'VE SEEN the movie *Hoosiers* know: It's the second-best David-beats-Goliath story in history, right behind, well, David and Goliath. And although the film contains made-up names and hyperbole-packed moments, the truth is in there: Tiny Milan High improbably *did* beat big-and-bad Muncie Central for the Indiana high school state basketball championship, on a buzzer beater by a kid named Bobby Plump.

For fifty-plus years, folks have turned Plump and his Milan teammates into Indiana dieties, the gods of Court Olympus. *The Indianapolis Star* named their victory the greatest sports moment in the state's history. The triumph has been used to argue against the class basketball playoff system now in place—no minor controversy in Hoosier-land. And, thanks to *Hoosiers*, those 1954 Milan Indians have given hope to every single underdog team in the sports world. (Just ask 'em.)

But what has been brushed over by the sands of history, covered up and buried in story-land, is that most-essential Goliath character in the tale—the Muncie Central Bearcats.

Indiana Basketball Hall of Fame director Roger Dickinson, has said: "Muncie Central's role in the game is not really important other than they lost. It could have been…any other big school; the significance would not be any different.

"Most folks," he added, "do not pay much attention to the losing team."

Well, Mr. Dickinson's just plain wrong.

Because no other team could have been any larger-than-life, could have been any more dominant, could have intimidated the crap out of Milan just by pulling up the team bus.

This is what the Milan kids—and any other opponent—knew when they stepped onto the court to face Muncie Central in 1954: The Bearcats had won 28 sectional titles, 16 regional titles, 10 semistate titles, and four state championships (more than any other Indiana school). They were the tallest squad in school history and one of the tallest in the state that year. They had won back-to-back championships in '51 and '52, and had lost to '53 Final Four participant Richmond in the regional. They were tabbed in a UPI state poll as the team to beat for the 1954 state championship. They were the definition of permanent success. And they knew it.

Jay McCreary, the Bearcats coach, said: "In Muncie, you never planned a basketball banquet until after the state finals. They expected you to do well all of the time. Some schools do well and then disappear. Muncie Central was consistent year in and year out."

McCreary had taken over just before the 1951-'52 season, and had brought in a running, up-tempo style of play. It was quite a change from Art Beckner, who had guided the school to a title in 1951 by playing a ball-control style. But Beckner left for more money at Richmond High, and McCreary knew he had been handed the luxury of great athletes at the big school. The talent pool was immense, and it produced a deep bench and a group of well-conditioned, intelligent, success-oriented players. The rise-to-the-top cream-of-the-crop, if you will.

The Bearcats were also hungry, because they had been knocked out of the '53 tourney by their former coach Art Beckner and his Richmond Red Devils, leaving them without a chance at the semistate or state trophies. It was an especially tough loss for three reasons: (1) It came at the hands of Beckner; (2) Muncie Central had already beaten Richmond twice in the regular season; and (3) the game agonizingly went into double-overtime. For the Bearcats' juniors—and for McCreary—the loss was their first in three IHSAA tournament appearances.

So the chance to play for the 1954 title meant something special to Muncie Central. The Bearcats were hungry, had something to prove, had the talent to back it up, and believed they could not be denied.

To start the tournament, Muncie Central had what many considered the easiest path to a regional championship. McCreary cautioned: "When you think you have an easy draw, that's when you get hit in the back of the head with a rock. There isn't any such thing as an easy draw."

But the games proved otherwise. McCreary's Bearcats beat up on Cowan, 89-38, then routed Daleville, 94-32, stomped on city rival Muncie Burris, 63-54, and whipped Union City in the regional opener. The only game that was even close came against Middletown, in the regional final, where Muncie Central had to overcome a 15-8 deficit to move on, 57-52.

Coach McCreary's fast-paced attack seemed to be gliding along on roller skates.

The semistate appeared, at first glance, to be a bit tougher. Top-ranked Fort Wayne North was up first, but Muncie Central disposed of them with ease, 62-48. Then, in the game that put them into the Final Four, the Bearcats roughed up unbeaten Mississinewa (27-0) by a 63-48 margin. Muncie Central went into the state finals scoring almost 70 points per game and triumphing by an average margin of 25.6 points.

At Butler Fieldhouse for the Final Four, the pairings broke down this way: Muncie Central vs. Elkhart in the morning game, followed by Milan vs. Terre Haute Gerstmeyer in the afternoon. Many coaches felt that the advantage went to the teams who played the first game, since they would have more time to rest for that night's championship match. Besides lack of recovery time, the winner of the second game also had less time to prepare a game plan.

In that first game, Elkhart took a 1-0 lead, and that was it: They never pulled in front again. Muncie Central breezed to a 59-50 victory, and found themselves only one win from redeeming the previous year's short tourney run.

In the second game, Milan defensed Gerstmeyer with a tight zone, daring Terre Haute to beat them with jump shots. They couldn't. Milan took a 29-23 lead into halftime and, after allowing Gerstmeyer to stick around for three-and-a-half quarters, closed the door for a 60-48 victory.

Still, the advantage in the championship leaned toward Muncie Central. Milan had not yet played the second game of a two-session tourney step and had to come back to play later that night. In both the regional and the semistate, the Indians won the first game of the morning session and had been better prepared and more rested than their opponents. In the evening's state final game, Muncie Central would be the well-rested team with the thorough game plan.

And that game plan was quite simple, really: Crash the boards hard, limit touches by Bobby Plump—far and away Milan's best player—extend the defense, and run, run, run.

Having a game plan is one thing. Executing it is something else entirely.

The Bearcats jumped out to an early 3-0 lead. But Milan tied the score at 7 and led 14-11 at the end of the first quarter. The game was not exactly a horse race, but it wasn't slow motion, either. Both teams struggled to find their legs and seemed to be worn down from the morning's battles. Muncie Central was especially sluggish, shooting only 19 percent in the first quarter and 30 percent in the second. Still, the game did not get away from them. Milan held a 23-17 lead at the intermission. But it could have been worse. It could have been much worse.

The Bearcats wasted no time in evening the score. Just after halftime they got two free throws and a long jumper to make it 23-21.

So Milan decided it was time to be a little more deliberate on offense. Okay, a lot more deliberate. In the entire third quarter, the Indians had managed to put just three points on the scoreboard, and the Bearcats had added just nine.

The game was tied.

So much for extending the defense and run, run, run. The Indians had thwarted the Central game plan by keeping their strong passing game working in overdrive and being careful with the ball. They worked it around for the good, high-percentage shot, and in doing so, prevented the Bearcats from running.

Muncie Central had kept Plump from doing too much damage, but he had scored 54 combined points in his two previous playoff games, and the Muncie faithful—as well as his hometown fans—fully expected him to be a factor in the fourth quarter of the biggest game of his life. The biggest game in the town's life, really.

To start the fourth, Muncie Central hit two quick free throws and pulled ahead 28-26. Now, most of the capacity crowd of 11,000-plus believed it would be a shootout to the finish, because Milan would have to keep pace and catch up.

This is where things stopped making sense.

This is what you don't see in the movie *Hoosiers*.

Milan coach Marvin Wood saw the game slipping away from his team. He knew they had been outscored 11-3 in the second half by the talented Bearcats. He knew Bobby Plump still hadn't found any kind of rhythm in his game. He knew that the one thing that could save his boys was not a giant miracle dropped from the rafters of Butler Fieldhouse, but the tiny pebble of an idea that wouldn't stop nagging at the back of his mind.

So Marvin Wood grabbed onto that pebble: He called timeout to adjust the game plan. Then he slung the pebble at the giant: He ordered his team to play cat-and-mouse—a decision that pretty much flew in the face of all accepted basketball wisdom.

Down by two, the game winding down, a more athletic, better rebounding, defensively patient team beating you, and you're going to...hold the ball? Are you nuts?

More than six minutes remained in the game, and Bobby Plump stood near halfcourt, the ball in his hands, waiting for his coach to say, "Go." It was surreal. The crowd got antsy. The tension mounted with every tick of the clock. And the Muncie Central fans knew that every minute that ticked off the clock was a step closer to their third title in the 1950s.

McCreary, sitting on the Central bench, couldn't believe what he was seeing. "I was wondering what he was going to do with it. We're two ahead, and he's standing out there holding the ball."

Said Wood: "If they weren't going to come and get us, we would just hold it. We would count on our experience beating their young kids at the end of the game."

Plump held the ball for one minute. Literally sixty seconds. The crowd got louder and louder. Then two minutes. Standing, keeping his pivot foot, looking his defender straight in the eye. Three minutes. How long could it go on? During the stall, his four teammates did exercises in the left corner of the floor. Forward Rollin Cutter said, "I really didn't know what to do. I just tried to stay out of the way."

Bobby Plump had plenty going through his mind. He was in the midst of his self-described "worst game of the tournament." He didn't want to make a mistake, to lose the ball. He wanted to trust his coach. He believed—like his coach—that if his team could stay within a couple of points, they had a legitimate chance to pull it out at the end. But mostly, he understood the stall was as bizarre a move as he'd seen on a basketball court. "I meet people all the time who say, 'I saw that game and I went to get a beer, and you were still standing there when I came back.'"

When the Indians finally went into their regular offense, the worst thing happened for them, and the best for the Muncie Central Bearcats: Plump missed his shot. It gave the Bearcats the ball back, and made ineffective the Milan stall. In fact, it cost the Indians dearly, as it took a chunk off the game clock and left them with less time to catch up.

But a sloppy pass gave the ball right back to the Indians.

With 2:12 left to play, Milan's Ray Craft tied the score with a short jumper.

Another Muncie Central turnover gave the Indians the ball again, and Bearcat sophomore Jimmy Barnes fouled Plump to send the senior to the line. He hit both free throws, and the Indians regained their lead, 30-28. Just 1:42 remained in the game.

Unbelievably, Muncie Central turned the ball over *again*, for the fourth time in the fourth quarter (somewhat remarkable considering how limited their possessions were as a result of the Plump stall). But Craft, just as unbelievably, missed a breakaway layup that could have sealed it, and Muncie Central had new life.

With forty-eight seconds remaining, John Flowers hit a running one-hander, tying the game at 30.

Plump got the ball safely in his hands and did just what his coach wanted him to: He held it for half a minute, until only eighteen seconds were left. Coach Wood called timeout.

Now, the film dramatized this part. There was no plan to fool Muncie Central, to use Plump as a decoy and let someone else take The Last Shot. Plump never had the chance to say, "I'll make it," as Jimmy Chitwood did in the huddle at the end of *Hoosiers*.

"We decided Plump was going to shoot," Wood said. "He was bigger than the player defending him, Jimmy Barnes. The big problem was what to do with the other players. Then [team captain Gene] White says, 'Why don't we just move all of the players away from center?'"

Sounded simple. Sounded good. Sounded like exactly the kind of thing Muncie Central would know was coming. "I tried to tell Jim [Barnes] not to go for his fake," said McCreary.

Those last eighteen seconds, Plump has been known to say, are the only things the movie was factual about. Which is good, because you couldn't make up anything better.

Coming out of the timeout, Plump received the ball at the top of the key. He held it for about thirteen seconds. Then, with five seconds to go, he made his move. *One dribble…two dribbles…jump stop…pump fake…Barnes goes for it…Plump lets 'er fly…and swish, through the hoop she goes.*

Of course, for Muncie Central, you couldn't make up anything worse.

There were still two or three seconds left when the ball dropped through, but nobody on Muncie Central could believe what had just happened. No one even thought to call timeout. Time kept on ticking, and the game ended.

Butler Fieldhouse erupted in joy. Much of the state of Indiana—watching on TV or listening to their radios, pulling for the underdog of all underdogs—shared the jubilation of the small-town boys from Milan. Parades were held, special days were declared, and Milan received a boost in tourism from folks who just wanted to see where the story originated.

But Muncie was a town torn. On the one hand, they had come so close. They had battled all the way to the championship game, and even though they couldn't celebrate a state championship, they could celebrate a season of successes. The kids lost, but they lost with class and dignity, the thinking went. The kids lost, but the loss was an incredible fluke, the thinking went even farther. Bob Barnet's column in the *Muncie Star* read, "Don't waste any sympathy on us Muncie folks. We'll get over that two-point near miss. We'll get well—we'll live. We'll get over it in a hurry."

On the other hand, there was no fluke. The Bearcats had choked. They had lost to a less-talented, less imposing group. They had fallen at the hands of a young coach with a pebble and scrawny kid with a slingshot. Herb Silverburg quoted Adlai Stevenson in the *Muncie Evening Press*: "'It hurts too much to laugh and I'm too old to cry.' That's the way Muncie felt Saturday evening."

• • •

There is an old black and white photo. It was taken just after Bobby Plump hit his last shot, capturing the moment out on the floor at Butler Fieldhouse. It, too, is truthfully portrayed in the film, broken down in surprising detail. The photo shows the Muncie Central players sitting on the gym floor, dejected, stunned, heartbroken. Their principal, a man named Loren Chastain, is trying to pick them up off the gym floor, almost pleading with them to hold their heads high. Their assistant coach, Carl Adams, is trying to do the same. The scene is pitiful, and if you look at it long enough, it's hard not to feel for those kids.

And the more you stare at the picture, the more you realize that Goliath was a human being.

2
DYNASTIES
AREN'T
FOREVER...
THANK GOD

THE YEARS: 1967-present
THE VENUE: Lamade Stadium in Williamsport, Pennsylvania
THE EVENT: The Little League World Series

TWELVE-YEAR-OLD heroes. When you sit down and think about it—really think about it—the Little League World Series has produced a surprising number of recognizable players. And not just recognizable to the seventh-grade sweethearts across the United States, but known by dads, uncles, grandmas, and readers of *Sports Illustrated* everywhere.

How can this be?

What makes 331,285 spectators show up at Howard J. Lamade Stadium in Williamsport, Pennsylvania, for a ten-day tournament of Little Leaguers?

Why would ABC Sports, ESPN and ESPN2 include *twenty-five games* on their schedules, broadcast to meet the demands of millions of viewers?

Why would we remember cheating Danny Almonte?

Why would we remember Chris Drury, not because he is an NHL All-Star, but because in 1989 he was featured on the cover of national magazines after he pitched his Trumbull, Connecticut, team past Taiwan for the Little League championship?

Why, every time we see Sean Burroughs playing third base for the San Diego Padres, do we imagine a chubby, 5-foot-5, 170-pound eleven-year-old who led his Long Beach, California, team to back-to-back titles in 1992 and '93, while hitting .600 and firing two no-hitters?

And why, oh why, do we remember Lloyd McClendon's most important career stat to be "five"—as in the five home runs in five official at-bats he hit for Gary, Indiana, in the 1971 Little League World Series?

What could possibly be the explanation for this fascination with pre-pubescents? Why would we, the American public, care so much about the outcome of a kiddie tournament that doesn't even involve our own kids or, most likely, any kids we know? And why would we have names and faces of past kid competitors burned into our memories?

Here's a theory: The Little League World Series is one of the last venues where the world's greatest Western superpower gets its butt kicked on a regular basis by the Far East.

To explain: The Little League World Series is broken up into four pools. The United States Regional Champions (from New England, West, Great Lakes, Gulf States, Mid-Atlantic, Northwest, Midwest, and Southeast) play in Pool A and Pool B. The rest of the world (broken down into Latin America, Caribbean, TransAtlantic, Asia, Pacific, Canada, Europe, and Mexico) squares off in Pool C and Pool D. What this round-robin system does is create a subtext of "We're so much more proficient than the rest of the world at baseball that we need to enter eight competitors into this tournament of champions and *assume* a spot in the final game." It also creates fantastic drama.

Because by the time the championship game rolls around, one American team emerges from the heap to face what has historically, for the most part, been the buzzsaw that is the Far East. And the American record versus said buzzsaw is, to put it nicely (we are, after all, talking about twelve-year-olds), not very good. To put it bluntly: We get our asses handed to us.

In fact, since 1967, when West Tokyo, Japan, won the Far East's first Little League World Series title, the United States has beaten a Far East contender for the championship five times. The Far East has won *twenty-four* head-to-heads against the U.S. In those games, the Far East has out-scored the United States 220-58. That's *two-hundred-and-twenty runs* in thirty-three games. It averages out to a little over seven per game.

The scoreboard doesn't lie. History doesn't lie. Both show that the United States has been thoroughly outplayed and outcoached in its own pastime by a group of outsiders from places like Taipei, Taiwan; Seoul, Korea; and

Osaka, Japan. This can be likened to a team of Pakistanis thoroughly dominating the World Curling Championships. Or the Dutch reigning as International Australian Rules Football Confederation champs for two decades. Or the United States men winning soccer's World Cup.

So the question becomes: How did the Far East youngsters get so dominant against American kids in the United States' pride-and-joy, baseball?

Discipline probably plays a factor. Not to say that America's kids aren't disciplined, but...America's kids aren't disciplined. Not enough. How many will field 200 ground balls a day? How many will take batting practice until they've worked out the loop in their swing? How many will memorize six different defenses against the bunt? How many know there *are* different ways to play a bunt? This is not to say American kids *should* spend so much time doing this stuff. It's just that the Far Easterners *are* spending the time, so when they beat you to a pulp, you can't be dumbfounded about it.

The second reason is a little more theoretical, and has a lot to do with geography, but stay with us, okay? America's best players are scattered all over the nation. There might be a great pitcher from Brownsburg, Indiana, and a fantastic power hitter from Tuscon, Arizona, and a magician-like shortstop from Trumbull, Connecticut. Then you've got a fast-as-lightning leadoff man that plays in San Diego, a fearless third-baseman from Gulf Shores, Alabama, and lefty curveball artist from Apopka, Florida. Well, each one of these dominant kids plays in a different region of the country. They can all make it to the Little League World Series—but they'd each be on a different team. Here's the difference: Taiwan, for instance, is considerably smaller than the United States (obviously). Think about this: Their six studs might all live in the same district. And if they don't already live in that district or city, maybe they take up residency for a while. It's no different than a U.S. family moving to a new school district so their son can play basketball for the best coach in the state. The Taiwanese know they can only send one team to the Little League World Series, and they also know that this is a way to make a name for themselves on a world stage (as silly as that sounds), so *why not* put all their best kids together and send them over to dominate an America that handicaps itself by splintering its best players?

Finally, it comes back to that spotlight. It comes back to the idea of twelve-year-old heroes, which is a silly notion to begin with. These kids *need* heroes, they shouldn't *be* heroes. But because the Little League World Series is played on American brickdust, and because it has turned into a media- and fan-friendly circus, with national reporters and ESPN coverage and Super Bowl-sized crowds, the pressure is ratcheted up. Ratcheted up pretty high for a kid whose whole family—nay, whole town or city—is watching each game he plays, calling him with congratulations when he wins, teasing him with barbs when he loses.

Kids are kids—they're going to make mistakes, they're going to commit errors. They *don't* take 200 grounders a day, or take two hours of batting practice in the cage. But when they know Harold Reynolds is going to be dissecting their strikeouts and booted ground balls on *Baseball Tonight*, they can't help but think about what the repercussions of each nuanced play might be. And that's when they play tight. And that's when they lose to all those other teams who aren't having to deal with the hometown beat writer, the *Sports Illustrated* photographer, the thirteen-year-old interviewer with the ABC camera crew, and the school bus full of hometown rooters *expecting* victory.

The reason we remember Lloyd McClendon, Sean Burroughs, Chris Drury, and Danny Almonte is because they were the exceptions; they rose above all the pressure and kid-ness of being an *American* twelve-year-old in the LLWS, and whupped some Far Eastern ass. When there's not very many, they're easy to remember. We hoist them up because they are in the teeny-tiny club who've been good enough to be carried off the field on our kids' shoulders. They're the rare American prepubescent winners.

Yes, the Far East has proven time and time again that it's pretty dominant when it comes to Little League baseball. That's partly because *they* know how to win. But it's also because *we* know how to lose. And losing plus fun equals growing up.

7

THE YEARS: 1970-1977
THE VENUES: Various NFL stadiums and Super Bowl sites
THE EVENTS: Important Minnesota Vikings games

FOLKS REMEMBER the Denver Broncos. And they sure as hell remember the Buffalo Bills. But when you talk about four-time Super Bowl losers, even die-hard sports fans tend to overlook The Purple Gang.

Yes, John Elway's Broncos were painfully overmatched in their four NFL championship games. And yes, Jim Kelly's Bills lost their four Super Bowls in a row. Since these wounds are fresh—having all occurred after 1978—Buffalo and Denver fans get to feel both proud and sorry (in a twisted, only-in-the-sporting-world kind of way) for their NFL teams.

But the Viking fans...their pain has been painted over. Purple-and-gold bleeding hearts covered up by orange and blue, and then blue and red.

It was on January 11, 1970, that the Vikings brought their vaunted Purple People Eater defense (led by linemen Alan Page, Carl Eller and Jim Marshall) and their balanced offense (powered by quarterback Joe Kapp, wide receiver Gene Washington, and running back Dave Osborn) to New Orleans' Tulane Stadium to take on the AFC's Kansas City Chiefs in Super Bowl IV.

The Purple People Eaters had a hard time stomaching Len Dawson, who came away with twelve completions in seventeen attempts, a 46-yard touchdown toss, and game MVP honors. The offense lost its balance, too, scoring only one touchdown and turning the ball over five times. The final score was 23-7, and needless to say, it wasn't much of a contest.

It was on January 13, 1974, that the Vikings made it back to the big game. This time, they brought more firepower, as state hero Fran Tarkenton—the team's first quarterback—returned after a four-year stint with the New York Giants. Well, okay, he was traded back to the Vikes in 1972, but this was his first trip to the Super Bowl. He was an All-Pro quarterback, and he greatly increased the team's offensive capability, which was a fantastic complement to its already strong D. Except in Super Bowl VIII, where neither side of the ball did many things right for Minnesota. The People Eaters couldn't stop the Miami Dolphins, who marched on two long first-period drives and scored a pair of touchdowns. Those two scores threatened to squash any Viking hopes. But Tarkenton led the offense to the Miami 7-yard line with 1:18 left in the first half.

Which is exactly where the Dolphins shut them down.

On second and third downs, Minnesota running back Oscar Reed picked up only one yard. On fourth-and-1 from the 6, Reed was crushed by Miami linebacker Nick Buoniconti and fumbled the ball—and the game—away. The Dolphins' Larry Csonka rushed thirty-three times for a Super Bowl-record 145 yards, keeping the Vikings' offense off the field and chewing up the clock. By the end, Minnesota had lost its second championship try, 24-7.

It was on January 12, 1975, that redemption was in the air. The Vikings returned to Tulane Stadium, site of their first Super Bowl appearance, to face the Pittsburgh Steelers.

The Steelers defense was built in the image of the Purple People Eaters—a tremendous front four, tackle-crazy linebackers, and smothering defensive backs. The two defenses proved their might in the first half, with the only score coming when the Steelers pummeled Tarkenton in his own end zone for a safety. With 4:27 left in the game, the Vikings had their best chance to win the Big Game yet when they blocked a punt and fell on the ball in the end zone. They trailed only 9-6. But again, hope was slowly tortured out of the Vikings, as Terry Bradshaw led Pittsburgh on an eleven-play, 66-yard drive, climaxing with a touchdown pass to Larry Brown. Final score: Pittsburgh 16, Minnesota 6.

It was on January 9, 1977, that the Vikings squared off against Oakland in front of 103,438 fans at the Rose Bowl and 81 million TV viewers worldwide—at the time the largest audience ever to watch a sporting event. Even though the Vikes had the public pulling for 'em, it wasn't enough. The Raiders gained a record 429 yards on offense, scoring on three consecutive second-quarter possessions to build a 16-0 halftime lead. Painfully, the Vikings could never quite mount a comeback, with Tarkenton throwing two fourth-quarter interceptions. The final score in this one was 32-16, and on that note, Minnesota had made its last embarrassing trip to the Super Bowl.

• • •

But that's not the end of the story.

As heart-rending as four Super Bowl losses might seem—when your team comes so close, one too many times, over and over again—that's not what really torments the Vikings' fans.

See, those Super Bowls can be excused. Let's face it: when your team is one of the best two in the league, it's hard to hold a grudge for too long. For these darker, drearier, less-forgiving scenes, you have to dig a little deeper. These are the ones that Viking faithful don't like to talk about. These are the ones that keep Vikings fans up at night, sweating, frustrated, bitter, miserable, and wondering why on earth they wouldn't just make it easy on themselves and become Packers' fans.

Recurring Nightmare Number 1: NFC divisional playoff game, 1975. The Vikings were coming off two Super Bowl losses in a row, which made them Big Game-hardened and hungry. They had begun the season with a ten-game winning streak, looking unbeatable in the process and cementing themselves as the favorite to win the NFL title. Fran Tarkenton had been rolling like he'd never rolled before, earning a *Sports Illustrated* cover shot with the caption, "He's Fran-tastic!" The team had scored more points than any other team in the NFC and had allowed the second-fewest.

So when they met the wild-card Cowboys in the first round of the playoffs, the Vikings were expected to follow Captain Fran-tastic's lead and roll some more.

But the game didn't work out that way. It was, in fact, a nail-biter, with the Vikings scoring late in the fourth quarter to grab a 14-10 advantage.

The Cowboys—and their outstanding quarterback, Roger Staubach—had one last chance. They made it to midfield, but with less than thirty seconds left in the game. Down by four, getting into field position wasn't good enough for the 'Boys; they needed a touchdown. Let's be clear: Covering 50 yards in less than thirty seconds is about as unlikely as the real Leif Erickson and a band of real Norsemen winning this year's America's Cup.

But there Staubach stood, in shotgun formation, his receivers out wide, his line prepared to throw themselves in front of a Mack truck to protect him. He got the snap. He pump-faked once to the center of the field. He turned to his right and launched a high, tight spiral down the sideline that seemed to hang in the air forever. There Cowboys receiver Drew Pearson glided, and just as the ball arrived, he shoved Viking defensive back Nate Wright. Wright fell, and got tangled up with safety Paul Krause, the only defender near enough to tackle Pearson. Pearson remained on his feet, calmly trapped the ball against his hip, and strolled easily into the end zone.

After the game, a reporter described the catch to Staubach, who had been knocked to the ground as soon as he threw the ball. Staubach's response: "It was just a Hail Mary pass; a very, very lucky play." It was the first time the phrase "Hail Mary" had ever been uttered in conjunction with a sports moment, but it wouldn't be the last. Especially where Minnesota Vikings are concerned.

Recurring Nightmare Number 2: NFC championship game, 1988. This Vikings squad was not particularly dominant. At least not in the regular season, where they had gone 8-7, scored exactly one more point than they had given up (336-335) and barely qualified for the postseason. But the playoffs were a different story.

Quarterback Wade Wilson found his rhythm and his sure-handed man—wideout Anthony Carter. The two led a nearly unstoppable attack that thoroughly dominated the Saints, 44-10. Even more impressive was the next weekend's game against the favored-to-win-the-Super-Bowl San Francisco 49ers, led by Golden Boy Joe Montana. The Vikings embarrassed the Niners, 36-24, in a performance that was not nearly as close as the final score indicated. The offense was again high-flying, and the defense sacked Montana four times and intercepted him twice. Both wins came on the road, in hostile environments.

So…going into the NFC title game, the Vikings were looking good. Very good.

The Redskins, their opponents, were a strong team—11-4 in the regular season. But, according to most analysts, they weren't any better than the Saints or the 49ers, both of whom the Vikings had disposed of with ease. Most thought the game would be a high-scoring shootout, and many were picking the Vikings to prevail.

But of course the actual contest played out oh-so-differently. By the fourth quarter of this grind-it-out defensive struggle, the Redskins led by only a touchdown, 17-10. The Vikings went on a long drive, all the way to the Redskins' 6-yard line. Roughly a minute remained in the game. It was four chances of "now-or-never."

On first down, the Vikings were stuffed. On second down, the Vikings were stuffed. On third down, stuffed again. And on fourth-and-goal, Darrin Nelson (one of the surest-handed running backs in the league, by the way) couldn't hold onto a catchable pass from Wade Wilson.

Agonizingly, the Vikings had gone with "never."

Recurring Nightmare Number 3: NFC Championship Game, 1999. This one's brutal, particularly because it involves the most dominant team in Vikings history. Nobody could stop the offense. Randall Cunningham, Robert Smith, and rookie sensation Randy Moss plowed the way to 556 regular-season points and a 15-1 record. They whipped the upstart Arizona Cardinals in a divisional playoff game, and met the balanced-but-not-explosive Falcons for the right to play in the Super Bowl.

With under five minutes left in the game, the Vikings led by a touchdown, 27-20. Better yet, they were in control of their own destiny, moving the ball down the field, driving all the way to the Atlanta 21-yard line. That's where the drive stalled, but there was nothing to fear: Kicker Gary Anderson was trotting onto the field to chip in a 38-yarder and put the game out of reach for the Vikings.

Up until that point in the season, Anderson had been literally automatic. Field goals: 39 for 39. Extra points: 67 for 67. The dude had attempted to put the ball through the goalposts 106 times in 1998-'99, and he'd been successful 106 times. The 38-yarder, in his home dome, with no weather conditions to screw him up, was a formality. The Vikings were going back to the Super Bowl for the first time since 1977.

Except, no. Because Gary Anderson missed kick number 107. It wasn't blocked. It wasn't a bad snap. He just missed it.

And with it, he cracked the door for the Falcons. Viking fans could feel 'em coming. Any second, they'd be plowing through, forcing themselves into the room that was the Super Bowl. With a quick touchdown, they did just that, forcing the game into overtime. Then, in sudden-death OT, the Falcons scored first, on a field goal by a kicker named Andersen—Morton Andersen.

And so it goes.

Recurring Nightmare Number 4: NFC Championship Game, 2001. In the biggest blowout in NFC Championship Game history (41-0), the Vikings were pounded, drubbed, hammered, sucker-punched, destroyed, or ruined—take your pick—by the New York Giants. In the final analysis, the Giants were on pretty equal footing, matchup-wise. It's hard saying what the hell happened, but...Who the hell knows?

Recurring Nightmare Number 5: The final regular-season game, 2003. The season started out 6-0. Six wins in a row. If you're an NFL franchise, that's nearly a sure indication you'll make the playoffs. It's almost certified.

Unless you're the Minnesota Vikings.

By season's end, the Vikes had managed to blunder their way to a 9-6 record, and they put themselves in a position where the last game was a must-win to even get into the playoffs. Luckily, that final game opponent turned out to be the hapless Arizona Cardinals. Just the reprieve the doomed franchise needed—a more-doomed franchise.

Unless you're the Minnesota Vikings.

These guys decided to use the game as a springboard to vault themselves as far past the Cardinals—and the Denver Broncos and the Buffalo Bills, for that matter—as they could, in terms of doomed-ness.

Sure, they led 17-6 in the fourth quarter. But that wasn't too big a lead to squander. Every Viking fan had to sit through one touchdown, which brought the game to 17-12 after a failed two-point conversion. Then, those same loyal fans—who'd given their hearts and souls to the purple-and-gold, despite what their heads said—had to watch the hapless Cards find their hap: They recovered an onside kick. They got help from a stupid pass-interference penalty against Minnesota. And a quarterback who nobody'd ever heard of—who's too unknown to even mention here (Okay, his name's Josh McCown. See? Ever heard of him?)—went bonkers, marching his team down to the 9-yard line.

Of course, the Cardinals teased the Vikings by allowing a sack, with McCown fumbling the ball all the way back to the 28-yard line. The haplesses-who-found-their-hap had no timeouts left, and by the time McCown assembled everyone for the snap, just two seconds remained on the game clock.

Of course, that's plenty of time when the Minnesota Vikings are involved, and their season's on the line, and there's a chance they can give their fans nightmares.

Of course, McCown coolly found Nathan Poole in the back corner of the end zone, zipped a prayer of a pass to him, and watched him catch the ball high above all the Viking defenders. Poole came down with one foot in the end zone, and one foot seemingly on the Vikings' throats.

Will the nightmares never end?

THE YEARS: 1981-present
THE VENUE: Staples Center (and an NBA arena near you)
THE EVENT: Each and every Los Angeles Clippers season

THERE USED TO be a club of "loser" franchises that we could all group together in our minds. Like the outcast table in the high school cafeteria, these were the teams—no matter what the league—who always got a lot of deserved attention on draft day.

You had the New Orleans Saints, with their twelve consecutive losing seasons in the '60s and '70s and their shamed-into-wearing-paper-bags-over-their-faces fans.

You had the New York Mets, with their first few baseball seasons of comedic error; they were funny in the same way that *Curb Your Enthusiasm* is funny—uncomfortably funny.

You had the Denver Nuggets, who spent a few years in the late '90s chasing the 1972-'73 Sixers for the worst single-season record in history; those Nuggets even went on a twenty-three-game tear of a losing streak.

You had the Tampa Bay Buccaneers, who annually found themselves in the NFC's basement—so far down they were always looking up at the almost equally loser-ish Detroit Lions.

You had the Texas Rangers, who'd never won a playoff series.

You had the Arizona Cardinals, who produced a winning percentage under .400 for their entire existence.

And you had the Los Angeles Clippers, basketball's most consistent team—as in consistently bad.

Something inevitably happened to the losers'club, though. They began to get up from the cafeteria table, one by one. The Mets were suddenly—there's never been a more appropriate use of the word than right there—Amazin'. They even won a World Series in 1986. The Ain'ts finally became the Saints, and forced their fans to remove the brown bags to watch them win a division title in 1991. The Cardinals made the playoffs behind hometown hero Jake "The Snake" Plummer for the first time in who-knows-how-long. The Nuggets drafted themselves a bona fide team-carrying superstar named Carmelo Anthony and, with him, the chance to be competitive for years to come.

And the Bucs…The Bucs played for the NFC Championship twice, but that wasn't all: They won the whole shebang, the Super Bowl, in 2003. (Which was sort of like quietly getting up from the outcast table, then dropping your tray with a bang so all the cool people are watching, turning around, and mooning the rest of the losers you just left behind.)

But one team never got up from the table.

The men in charge: general manager Elgin Baylor and owner Donald Sterling.

Baylor is widely regarded as one of the great talents in NBA history. Selected to the NBA's fifty Greatest list in 1996, he's also, arguably, the greatest player to *never* win a championship. The season after he retired trophy-less, the Lakers won a record thirty-three games in a row and rolled to their first-ever NBA title.

Sterling, a Los Angeles-area real estate mogul with a rep for penny-pinching and meddling, took over the former San Diego Clippers in 1981. The team drew the fewest fans in the league and was up to its rec specs in debt. Sterling promised to remake the team in his own image and even plastered billboards of himself all over town. "It's the start of a new era!" he promised. "I'll build the Clippers through the draft, free agency, trades, spending whatever it takes to make a winner."

This was the same owner who later reportedly asked head coach Paul Silas if the players really needed a trainer that much. And then asked Silas if *he* would mind taping his own players before the games.

Another example: Just after Sterling bought the team, he invited prominent San Diego lawyers and real estate agents to lunch to meet his new players. He set up a free-throw shooting contest, with a reward: Win and take home $1,000. A lawyer named Michael Spilger—who'd played basketball at San Diego State in the late '60s—made nine out of ten to win the contest. But he was told soon afterward that the prize offer had been rescinded. The new prize would be five days in Puerto Rico—not including airfare, transportation, or food. Spilger told Sterling he'd take the $1,000.

According to Spilger, Sterling replied, "How about double or nothing?"

Spilger didn't acquiesce. And Sterling asked if he'd settle for two season tickets.

He wouldn't. And two weeks later, Spilger got a letter congratulating him for winning top prize—three days and two nights in Vegas.

Spilger sued the Clippers for fraud.

At the 1982 home opener, Sterling forced a team official to track down Spilger and offer a compromise: a $1,000 donation to his favorite charity. "I'll see you in court," Spilger said. And two days later—a year after he sank his free throws to win the contest—he finally got his grand.

That's not penny-pinching. That's…something scarier. And it's the kind of thing that would kill the morale of a group of players, that would hurt your chances of attracting quality free agents, that would undercut any fan loyalty that might be developing.

But it was only the first indication of a pattern of scrimpiness that would grow by leaps and bounds. In season two, Sterling proposed to slash training camp expenses from $50,000 to $100. He also wanted to reduce the scouting budget from $20,000-plus to $1,000, the advertising expenses from $200,000 to $9,000, and medical expenses from $10,000 to $100.

The point of all these "Donald Sterling is a cheapskate" stories is not to tear down the man, but to emphasize: In sports, there is a link between the willingness to spend some money and winning ballgames. Ask George Steinbrenner. Ask Theo Epstein. Ask Mark Cuban.

Don't ask Donald Sterling.

Because he'll tell you that he wants to win—that he's always wanted to win so badly. He once said, "How do I cope? It's very hard. I've suffered. Oh, how I've suffered…The pain, the torment, the absolute torture! How do the owners of the Chicago Cubs get through it?" But records are records. And the records show that the Clippers have made the playoffs just three times since Donald Sterling took the helm. Their best won-lost mark has been 45-37. Their worst has been 12-70. (That's a winning percentage of .146.) In 1999-'00, they managed to win only fifteen games. In *four* other seasons during Sterling's tenure as owner, they eked out just seventeen wins.

Donald Sterling might say he wants to win, but the fact is, he never has. And he's done nothing to back up his statements.

It shows mostly in his payroll. Sterling has kept his salary spending within the lowest five in the league since he's owned the Clippers. There were years when it amounted to half the dollars the Lakers were paying players. Elton Brand is the first player Sterling's Clippers ever signed to a maximum deal, and that was in 2003. Before then, the most The (Other) Donald had ever doled out was $4 million for one player's season services. (This fact is remarkable when you consider Michael Jordan once made $33 million in a season for the Chicago Bulls; in the salary-cap era, Rasheed Wallace makes $17 million per season and Antoine Walker $13.5 million. And those guys aren't even the best players on their respective teams.)

Sterling's spending philosophy is no secret. Ron Harper—one of the few big ticket free agents the Clips re-upped in the '80s and '90s—put it thusly: "Cash is the root of all evil, and Sterling likes to hold onto his. He won't hand it out to a player unless he thinks the player has earned it."

But there's the problem: the rest of the NBA doesn't work like that. Players are regularly overpaid. Weak-kneed backup centers make $4 million. Simply put: Teams that want to win…pay. And teams that don't care about winning…don't.

Carl Scheer—Clippers G.M. from 1984 to 1986—summed it up: "I don't know how important winning is to Donald. He seems more concerned that his books are balanced, that he runs one of the few NBA franchises with no debt, that he can bring his friends to games." Which is nice, because there are a lot of empty Staples Center seats for those friends to choose from.

But the Clippers' problems aren't all about the benjamins. There's also the matter of the Benjamins—as in Benoit Benjamin, poster child for all that has gone wrong with the Clippers' roster over the last twenty-plus years.

Benoit Benjamin was a 7-footer coming out of college, in the 1985 draft; he played for a small school—Creighton—in a below-average conference. His stats were impressive, but remember, he put them up in a league that didn't have many guys to match up with him. So...the Clippers used their number-three pick to select Benjamin. There were other guys they could have drafted. Chris Mullin. Karl Malone. Joe Dumars. Detlef Schrempf. A.C. Green. But, no. Benoit Benjamin was their man.

Benjamin went on to have a perfectly ordinary career for the Clips. He lasted just five-and-a-half seasons in L.A. He averaged about 13 points and 8 rebounds per game. Not such bad numbers. Until you consider: When the Clippers drafted Benjamin, they were coming off four straight seasons of less than thirty-one wins. They needed a stud. They got a utilitarian journeyman who would lead them to horrendous twelve-, seventeen-, twenty-one-, and thirty-win seasons, then go on play for *nine* more NBA teams. (For sake of comparison, a kid named Michael Jordan was the number-three pick in the draft the year before Benoit Benjamin.)

This is the sort of luck the Clippers created with their draft picks, free agent acquisitions, and other personnel moves. At this point, G.M. Elgin Baylor has to take some of the heat. Because he's the one with the job description that includes drafting young players, acquiring free agents, and making other personnel decisions.

Benoit Benjamin was typical of Baylor's and Sterling's draft results, but he was nowhere near the worst. In 1987, the Clippers had the fourth pick and chose Reggie Williams; Scottie Pippen and Reggie Miller were selected just behind Williams. In '89, the Clippers held the second pick, which they used to take Danny Ferry; Glen Rice was selected just behind him.

At the top of the bad draft list has to be 1998, when the Clippers had the top pick and used it on Michael Olowokandi, a 7-footer from a small school—Pacific—in a below average conference. (Sound familiar?) Here are some other names the Clippers overlooked in that same draft: Mike Bibby, Antawn Jamison, Dirk Nowitzki, Paul Pierce. All have been cornerstones of their own NBA franchises. Excepting, of course, Olowokandi, who developed into a second-rate center and got out of L.A. A.S.A.P.

Owner Sterling has said, "I'm only as good as my advisors." And if that's true, then the next question has to be, "Why don't you change your advisors?" Well, he has an answer: "Loyalty to my G.M. I like Elgin, I respect him and trust him. I want to see him succeed. Some people think the solution to everything is change. I like continuity."

That's a valid sentiment, except that whole thing about trust and respect and wanting to see the guy succeed, etc., isn't true. If you look a little deeper, you'd notice that Sterling clipped Baylor's wings many, many times. The best example came in '93, when Baylor had a trade all worked out with the Miami Heat. He was going to send the Clippers' star forward, Danny Manning—who had a year left on his contract and was hinting he would leave—to the Heat for their even-better star forward, Glen Rice, and Willie Burton. Sterling would not allow the trade and was certain he could convince Manning to stay in L.A. After four months, Sterling gave up, realizing Manning could not be convinced. But the Clippers had missed their opportunity with Rice. In an attempt to get something, anything, for Manning—instead of watching him leave via free agency, which offered no return on investment—they sent the twenty-seven-year-old to Atlanta for thirty-four-year-old free-agent-to-be Dominique Wilkins. Wilkins played out the year, then rejected a half-assed offer from Sterling, and skipped town. The Clippers were left with nothing in return for Manning, who had been their only bona fide star player at the time.

Time and time again, the Los Angeles Clippers have been left with nothing—mostly from their own unwillingness to pay respectable salaries; or their own uninformed draft choices; or their own downward spiral of mismanagement that starts with leader-of-the-pack Donald Sterling, filters through G.M. Elgin Baylor, and spreads from team to team, player to player, Benoit Benjamin to Michael Olowokandi.

So...you really couldn't blame Elgin Baylor when he didn't even bother showing his face at the 2004 Draft Lottery.

Maybe he finally felt too much shame. Maybe he finally was fed up with being the face of a feckless organization. Maybe he was finally tired of holding the torch for all the teams who had bowed out of the club through the years, leaving the Clippers as the last loser standing.

THE YEARS: 1991-1998
THE SCHOOL: Prairie View A&M, located 45 miles from Houston in southeastern Texas
THE EVENT: Eighty games

"I'LL PROBABLY go down as one of the worst coaches that's ever been."

Ronald Beard said it, and it's hard to disagree with him. He led—or, maybe, dragged—Prairie View A&M's football program to forty-four consecutive losses—the longest losing streak in NCAA Division I-AA history. And that's where his record stood—0–44—when Beard was fired in 1995. A winning percentage of .000.

Beard is not alone when it comes to percentage. Hensley Sapenter went winless during his term. So did Fred Freeman. The difference is, Sapenter only lasted one year, and Freeman only two. Beard made it through four.

The shameful streak actually started in 1989, when the Panthers lost their last two games of the season. Then came the first knockdown: The Prairie View brain trust suspended football for the entire 1990 season after uncovering a financial scandal within. Apparently, money had been mismanaged by some members of the athletic department. The football team became the martyr, with hopes that a year's hiatus would be enough for a regroup and reinvention.

The program came back the following season—1991—and that's when Beard took the reins—with, admittedly, some major challenges. Because of a shortage of funds (due—not surprisingly—to the financial scandal), there were no scholarships to be had. Kinda made it tough to recruit talented kids when every other school in the conference gave its players money to participate.

The first year back from the suspension was the most embarrassing. In that 1991 season, the Panthers eked out just 48 points during the entire season. Meanwhile, their opponents *averaged* 56 per game. Ever heard the phrase "winning ugly?" The 1991 Prairie View squad was *losing* ugly.

It didn't get any better the next year. Loss piled upon loss, leading to the supreme kick in the face: In the sixth game of the season (and number seventeen of the streak), the Panthers met up with West Texas State, itself riding a nine-game losing streak and in its first revival season after a year off. It was a clash of whatever's-the-opposite-of-titans; the winner got to end its losing streak.

The game was close, which, in itself was something of a moral victory for Prairie View A&M. Unfortunately, the way it lost was the twist of the knife. Duane Joubert ran back a 94-yard kickoff return for a touchdown. The same Joubert had recently transferred to West Texas from Prairie View.

Ouch.

The worst part of such a long losing streak must have been the breaking of each successive "longest losing streak" record. Number forty-five happened to be Beard's penultimate game, the second-to-last of the 1994 season. That loss broke the previous Division I-AA record, held by Columbia, which recorded an "L" in every game from November 12, 1983 to October 8, 1988. Prairie View's number fifty-one broke the all-time college mark, held by Division III Macalester (out of Minnesota), whose own streak ended on September 6, 1980.

You've got to think that, as a Prairie View player or a coach, it was more than a little disheartening to have seen such milestones in the rearview mirror. Makes you wonder why they kept going out there.

Truth be told, in some cases they didn't.

Ian Smith, a player on the 1995 team, explained: "We have practice at four o'clock, and you might have six people out there. The team has like seventy-something members, but you have only six show up. Then when the time comes to make up the travel squad for a road game, everybody comes back out again, ready to go."

Greg Bell, class of '96, said: "When they miss practice, they're either off studying somewhere or hiding in their rooms. Mostly hiding in their rooms."

Of course, it's hard to blame them. These were kids playing for no real reason—at least not one that could be observed. Not even pride. They didn't receive scholarships. Nobody—well, nearly nobody—came to see their home games. And if they did, it was only to take in the award-winning halftime performance of the band. Once intermission was over, the crowds would scatter and be gone.

The athletic department gave them no real funding—not even to buy practice jerseys. The Panthers wore hand-me-downs from the Houston Oilers.

Worse, some of the large lineman never had shoulder pads big enough to fit. "What they have is like peewee league shoulder pads," says 300-pounder Dedric Clark, who ended up transferring to Iowa Wesleyan in 1995. "We had better equipment in high school. And something else: At Prairie View they don't even use washing powder to do our laundry. They wash the uniforms in water, nothing else." Not only were Prairie View players embarrassed as hell for their streak...they stunk, too.

Once the losses added up to record-setting proportions, observers fell into one of two camps: those who felt great sympathy for the Panthers, and the rest.

The rest began piling on.

Graduated teammates didn't want current Panthers to win because *they* never did. Referees were heard—on the field—to chide, "Man, what do y'all think y'all are doing out here?"

For the first time maybe in history, band members disparaged football players.

It went the same way with cheerleaders.

"We were coming to practice one night before a game with Texas Southern," recalled Benjamin Goffney, a free safety on the '95 team, "and we were walking and [the cheerleaders] blocked our way and started calling us sorry and saying, 'When are y'all going to win a game?' and stuff like that. They were so mad they wanted to fight. They treated us like a bunch of dogs—like we wanted to lose. Man, we don't want to lose!"

To gain a full understanding of the depths to which Prairie View sank, it's helpful to note this: Not one, not two, not even three...but four— *four!*—classes of seniors went through their playing careers at the school without winning even one game.

By 1998, the Panthers program had reached the apex of lowness: Eighty. Subtract thirty from it and Prairie View would *still* hold the record for most consecutive losses in college football history. Four coaches had come and gone during the streak, unable to break the hard-luck karma. Plenty of different schools had occupied a place on the Prairie View schedule, many of them cupcakes—the better to break the curse against. None would play the role properly.

Finally, along came Langston.

Langston had begun the streak back in 1989, the year before the one-year hiatus. The Panthers newest coach, Greg Johnson, had left Langston in 1996 to rebuild at Prairie View.

There was a change in the karmic force that late-September Saturday in 1998 when Johnson's old school marched into Blackshear Field to face his new team.

It couldn't have been more dramatic. The game was tight down to the final minute, a 14-12 defensive battle in Prairie View's favor. At least that's what the scoreboard said when Langston scored with 34 seconds left in the game. But they still had one chance to tie and send it to overtime, and then deliver Prairie View to its eighty-first consecutive loss. There was a two-point conversion to be played, with basically no time left on the clock.

Prairie View lined up on defense, so close to the taste of victory they *needed* it. Langston lined up on offense, surprised—and somewhat embarrassed—to even be in this dramatic situation.

The play was called.

Running back Archie Craft got the ball, scampering straight up the middle.

And that's where Prairie View's Steven Garner stopped him—and the awful eighty-game losing streak—dead in its tracks.

3

THE WHOLE
WORLD IS
WATCHING:
THE OLYMPICS

THE YEAR: 1912
THE VENUE: Stockholm, Sweden
THE EVENT: The Olympic Games' decathlon and pentathlon

TAKE AWAY Jim Thorpe's athletic ability, and you're left with one of the saddest lives you'll ever hear about.

Born in 1887, in the Oklahoma Indian Territory called Prague. Father came from Sauk and Fox and Irish heritage. Mother came from Potawatomi and French ancestors. Described himself as "an American Airedale."

Born with a twin brother, Charlie. Inseparable. Wrestled. Swam. Ran. Climbed. Jumped. Competed. Jim usually got the best of Charlie. Then they turned nine. Pneumonia got the best of Charlie.

Turned to his father to compensate. Hunted bear. Tamed wild colts. Fished with long spears. Competed. But not against each other—against nature. Didn't want to beat his dad; wanted to be just like his dad.

Sent away to Indian school in Lawrence, Kansas, for a change of scenery. Got word dad had been shot in a hunting accident. Rushed home to Oklahoma. While there, watched mother die from labor complications.

Wedge driven between father and son. Son left for Texas. Trained horses and worked odd jobs. Got his mind right and returned home to father with self-trained team of horses.

Turned sixteen. Announced to dad that he wanted to attend the Carlisle Indian Industrial School in Pennsylvania. Soon as he got there, received word his dad died. Grieved horribly. Still wanted to be just like his dad.

Turned twenty-six. Got married to Carlisle sweetheart. Turned twenty-

eight. Became father to James, Jr. Turned thirty-one. Watched his own three-year-old die from long sickness. Turned to drinking.

Divorced Carlisle sweetheart after ten years and three daughters. Remarried two years later and scrounged his way through the Great Depression. Painted gas stations and worked as a laborer for $4 a day.

Depression came and went. Time moved on. Second wife moved on. Third wife moved in. Body began to break down after years of physical labor and hard drinking. Surgery on cancerous growth, lower lip. Finally, a third heart attack took his life.

Sad. Wretchedly sad.

• • •

Except there's a piece that's been left out.

There's a talent that's been given, and a talent that's been used, and a talent that's been rewarded.

It was Jim Thorpe's talent, and that talent is this: The guy was the greatest athlete of his era.

A good argument can be made he is the greatest athlete of all time.

And, in a life bulging with tragedy, this one tremendous thing cannot be overlooked: Jim Thorpe's undeniable ability led him to the most satisfying moment in his—hell, in any competitor's—lifetime.

It started on the Oklahoma plains with Charlie, his twin. That's where Thorpe learned to love games, love competition, strive to be better than the next guy (who happened to be a mirror of himself). It continued in the wilderness with his father. That's where Thorpe learned to love the idea of teammates, love cooperation, love working with a teacher and coach. It blossomed at Carlisle, in Pennsylvania, with a coach named Pop Warner. That's where Thorpe learned to love dominance, love the structure of athletic competition, love football and baseball.

There was an important moment at Carlisle, one that happened—to the surprise of everyone in Thorpe's circle—on the track-and-field oval. Jim had stopped to watch the varsity team practice high jumping. The kids easily cleared 5'6". Then 5'7". Finally, 5'8". But when the bar was raised to 5'9", not one of them could get over it. They kept knocking it down: clang, clang, clang.

That's when Thorpe asked to give it a try.

Everyone thought it would be a funny sight, this football player in his tennis shoes and overalls jumping through the high jump bar. But that's not what happened. In fact, Thorpe cleared the bar easily, and in the process set the school record.

Without spikes; wearing overalls.

Pop Warner saw the whole thing and realized Thorpe's potential, as a natural athlete, to dominate track and field events. When pressed into service, the youngster did not disappoint. He excelled on the track and on the gridiron, and Warner pointed out: "He weighed around 178 and was an exceptionally well-built athlete. He had speed as well as strength."

But when his enrollment at Carlisle ended in the spring of 1909, Thorpe had to move on. He was flat broke.

He learned from a couple of classmates that he could make a living playing semipro baseball in North Carolina. The three schoolboy friends traveled to Rocky Mount and spent the summer playing for $15 a week.

Thorpe enjoyed it so much that, after a winter spent back home in Oklahoma, he returned to the Carolina semipro league for the 1910 summer season. His statistics weren't great. As a pitcher his first season, he went 19-20 with the Rocky Mount Railroaders, a sub-.500 team. And playing for the Fayetteville Highlanders in 1910, he batted .250 in eighty-nine games. The fact was, baseball wasn't football (Thorpe's first love) or track and field (his second). He hadn't practiced the game much. But it was a sport. And Thorpe—in his simple way—knew it didn't get any sweeter than being paid to play a game.

In 1911, Pop Warner contacted Thorpe, asking him to return to Carlisle as a student. But Warner also had bigger plans: He wanted Thorpe and classmate Louis Tewanima to train for the 1912 Olympics, to be held in Stockholm, Sweden.

The young Indians trained for months, and in the end, both made the U.S. Olympic team. Tewanima would go as a distance runner. Thorpe would try to pull off a ridiculously challenging double—competing in the decathlon *and* pentathlon.

In the track and field pentathlon (different from the modern pentathlon—still in existence today—which consists of swimming, pistol shooting, running, fencing, and horse riding), Thorpe pulled off the incredible: He took first in four events—the broad jump, the discus, the 1,500-meter run, and the 200-meter dash—and third in the javelin. He won the gold medal with a score of seven. In this event, where the low score wins, the silver medalist wound up with twenty-one.

This set Thorpe up very decidedly as the favorite in the grueling ten-event decathlon. If only he could survive it.

He started out by winning the shot put.

Then he won the high jump with a leap of 6', 1.6".

He finished the 110-meter hurdles in 15.6 seconds, which turned out to be a record unbroken until Bob Mathias came along *thirty-six years* later.

On the last day of the decathlon, Thorpe set a personal best in winning the 1,500 with a time of 4:40.1. This gave him 8,412 out of a possible 10,000 points (higher is better this time), breaking the world record by an absurd 998 points, and distanced him from runner-up Hugo Wieslander of Sweden by 688 points. Where others had dropped out from tortured exhaustion (a competitor named Avery Brundage withdrew from the decathlon after taking sixth in the pentathlon), Thorpe not only survived... he dominated.

When Thorpe was presented his gold medal for the decathlon, it was by the King of Sweden, Gustav V, who also threw in a jewel-encrusted miniature Viking ship and a life-size bronze bust of the Swedish royal himself. The King placed the medal around Thorpe's neck, and as he did so, said: "Sir, you are the greatest athlete in the world."

Thorpe—in his way—replied: "Thanks, king."

There had never been an athlete so incredibly versatile, so effortlessly competitive, so thoroughly dominant. No one had ever seized hold of a moment so big—with the whole wide world watching—and wrung the moment's neck until every last drop of drama and success and sweetness was squeezed out.

Jim Thorpe returned to the States flying higher than any U.S. athlete had ever flown. He was a worldwide sensation; he was an American hero.

But in January 1913, Thorpe lost his wings.

The Amateur Athletic Union (AAU) discovered that he had played semipro baseball during the summers of 1909 and 1910. He was paid for his services, and no matter how much (or little) it might have been, they ruled that this action broke their sacred Olympic amateurs-only rule.

The organization stripped Thorpe of his wins, literally collecting the gold medals from him, along with the ribbons, trophies and even the bronze bust and bejeweled Viking ship.

If he weren't such a simple, honest man, Thorpe would have done what was common practice in those Carolina semipro leagues: He would have used a fake name, so as not to jeopardize his amateur status.

If he weren't such a simple, honest man, Thorpe would have argued: "Wait. I played semipro baseball. I competed in a whole different sport in the Olympics, and maintained amateur status in that. Not to mention, baseball isn't an Olympic sport at all."

If he weren't such a simple, honest man, Thorpe wouldn't have turned himself in to the AAU in the first place; he wouldn't have humbled himself in the public eye and begged for the organization's forgiveness (even though most major sportsmen and the American public supported his side of things).

Within the next year, Thorpe could be found playing outfield for the New York Giants. He never made much of a fuss about losing his medals, never complained about the public humiliation, never held news conferences to tell his side of the story—all the stuff you see superstar athletes doing today.

But his roommate with the Giants, a fellow Indian named Chief Meyers, told of one truthful night: "Very late, Jim came and woke me up...He was crying, and tears were rolling down his cheeks. 'You know, Chief,' he said, 'the King of Sweden gave me those trophies. He gave them to me. But they took them away from me. They're mine, Chief. I won them fair and square.'"

But that's not the saddest thing.

No, the saddest part of this tale comes later, much later, after a pro baseball career and a pro football career and time spent wearing an Indian headdress, touring the country for speaking engagements. The sad part comes after the three marriages and the seven children and the body that begins to fall apart. The sad part comes after a lifetime of campaigns mounted on Thorpe's behalf—to have his good name and his medals and his records returned to him—and a lifetime of campaigns that failed.

In the end, the International Olympic Committee would not give back Thorpe's medals. To add insult to injury, an aristocratic and sanctimonious man named Avery Brundage became the head of the AAU in 1933, then the IOC in 1952, and adamantly maintained that Thorpe's ignorance of the definition of amateur was no excuse for his decision to accept payment to play baseball.

Further, he maintained that the IOC would never relent on this position while he was its leader.

And Brundage was true to his word. (If you're wondering why the name sounds familiar, it's because this is the very same Avery Brundage who finished sixth behind Jim Thorpe in the 1912 Olympic pentathlon, and couldn't find the strength or courage Thorpe did to complete the decathlon.)

Jim Thorpe died in 1953, never laying eyes on his hard-won gold medals again. He never got to hold the miniature Viking ship that was taken from him in 1913. He never had the pleasure of flipping through a book of records and seeing his name in it, under "Olympics: Track and Field." All these things were lost, pried from a life already full of tragedy.

Finally, in 1973—a full twenty years after Thorpe died and one year after Avery Brundage stepped down as IOC chair—the AAU retroactively restored Thorpe's amateur status. It was a significant hurdle that had been overcome, since it was the AAU that had denied Thorpe his records and trophies in the first place.

Nearly ten years later—in 1982—Thorpe's accomplishments were restored in the Olympic record book.

Soon after, each of his seven children was presented with replicas of his two gold medals by the IOC.

Jim Thorpe's place in history is now forever assured: He was the greatest athlete of the first half of the twentieth century. And his family has the medals to prove it. But the man lived a lifetime lost without those same validations.

11

THE YEAR: 1936
THE VENUE: Olympic Stadium, Berlin, Germany
THE EVENT: The XI Summer Olympiad

IT STANDS TO reason that most losers in the world of sports are athletes. Oh, sure, there are managers and team owners who earn that moniker, but the majority of sports losers are the men and women who are actually out there failing to put points on the scoreboard, trailing in the race, missing the putts or dropping the ball.

Occasionally, though, the loser is someone who isn't in the competition.

In 1936, that person was Adolf Hitler.

Now, on paper, Hitler and his German team did very well at the Berlin games. They dominated, in fact. Consider that in the prior six Summer Olympics, Germany had won a total of twenty-eight gold medals. In 1936 alone, Germany won thirty-three. They took home (home being pretty close), eighty-nine gold medals, their highest ever—and the highest of any country that year. The United States was a distant second with fifty-six.

So what made Germany's leader a loser?

A guy named Jesse Owens.

Born James Cleveland Owens, this son of a sharecropper and grandson of slaves first raised eyebrows when his gym teacher timed him in the 60-yard dash and offered to train him before school. (After school didn't work out because Owens had a job carrying groceries.) He quickly became a track star at Cleveland East Technical High and was recruited by, among others, Ohio State—where, despite his exceptional skills, he still had to face what just about every African-American at the time was facing—segregated apartments, "blacks-only" restaurants and hotels, back doors, and stairways.

In 1935, he set three world records and tied a fourth in the course of forty-five minutes at a Big Ten meet, a feat that made it clear that he should be part of the Olympic trials. There, he placed first in the 100-meter and 200-meter sprints, assuring him a spot on the team.

A little context might be important before we get into the Olympics. While Adolf Hitler's rise to power in Germany had caused concern in America, the two countries were not at war. But there was a psychological war going on, as Hitler and company set out to prove that the "racially pure" Aryans were superior to anyone on the planet.

From Hitler's perspective, this had already been established a few months before the games. That's when boxing great Max Schmeling, the most famous German in America—except, perhaps, Hitler himself— knocked out Owens' friend Joe Louis (in a fight Schmeling had arranged without Hitler's approval—the Fuhrer was reportedly shocked at the arrangement, fearing that Louis, an African-American, might land a humiliating victory). What to Schmeling was a one-on-one athletic competition, was to his country's leader a sign of racial dominance.

As the games commenced in Berlin, Schmeling himself visited Owens while touring Olympic Village and proved remarkably courteous. Historian Donald McRae, in his book about Lewis and Owens, *Heroes Without a Country*, quotes Schmeling as saying, "Coming back to Germany, I looked forward to three things. One was to see my wife, two was to do a little hunting, and three was to see you win some gold medals."

"Max is all right," Owens later commented. "But Joe'll whip him next time."

But what about this time, for Owens, on the track? To say that he was under pressure is a gross understatement. Approximately 50,000 spectators packed the Olympic stadium. And while television coverage had yet to be part of the games, filmmaker Leni Riefenstahl's camera operators seemed to be everywhere as she shot footage for *Olympia*, a documentary masterpiece that would fuel "Is it propaganda or is it not?" debates that continue to this day.

The German crowd chanted Owens' name as he jogged around the parimeter of the track, surely disconcerting for someone expecting a hostile reception. Still, in his first run at the 100-meter sprint, he matched the world record of 10.3 seconds. Later in the day—with Hitler, Goering, Goebbels and Himmler now in attendance—Owens topped his previous run by a tenth of a second, setting a world record (a record that would later be termed "wind-assisted" and, therefore, not counted). The crowd—not including Adolf and company—stood to cheer.

The next day, in the finals, Owens took his first gold medal with another 10.3 second run. As Hitler watched, a wreath of laurel was placed on Owens' head and a potted oak from the Black Forest was given to him as a gift of the host country. The previous evening, after Hitler had shaken hands with German winners but was nowhere to be found when African-American high jumpers Cornelius Johnson and Dave Albritton took the gold and silver, International Olympic Committee prez Henri Baillet-Latour reportedly met with him to strongly suggest he shake hands with either all or none of the winners.

No hands would be shaken as, on day three, Owens ran for identical times—21.2 seconds—in both of his 200-meter heats and became the first Olympic long jumper to land farther than twenty-six feet, defeating German favorite Lutz Long. In another sign of athletes transcending politics, the silver medalist congratulated the gold, forming a bond that would lead to long conversations in the Olympic Village. They formed a quintessentially Olympic friendship, rendered more poignant by the statements being made by German officials (i.e. references to "nonhumans like Owens and other Negro athletes").

Hitler shook no hands the next day, either, as Owens scored his third gold medal by running the 200-meter finals in 20.7 seconds.

That should have been the end of it. But in a last-minute switch, the U.S. team's coaches subbed Owens and Ralph Metcalfe for Jewish relayers Marty Glickman and Sam Stoller, a move Owens reportedly objected to and that led to accusations of anti-Semitism on the part of the coaches.

Whatever the reason, the move meant that Owens would win his fourth gold medal as the quartet finished with a full fifteen-yard lead.

It also meant that Owens became the first Olympic athlete ever to win four gold medals.

It meant that while for the Americans the war was still five years away, Jesse Owens had scored a decisive victory.

And that Adolf Hitler—not the German athletes he bested, and not the Filipino, Portuguese, or Australian teams that each took home only a single bronze medal—was the biggest loser at the games.

12

THE YEAR: 1972
THE VENUE: Munich, West Germany's basketball forum
THE EVENT: The Olympic gold medal basketball game, United States vs. Soviet Union

WITH SIX SECONDS left, the streak was just about dead. Not quite, but just about.

The players—the Americans and the Soviets—knew it.

The coaches—Henry Iba and Aleksandr Gomelskii—knew it.

The world knew it.

The United States had never lost an Olympic basketball game. Never. Sixty-three and oh. Gold medal. Gold medal. Gold medal. Gold medal. Gold medal. Gold medal. Gold medal. Count 'em up. Seven. And nothing else. No silver. No bronze. No "Did Not Place."

The U.S.A. had the upper hand over *the rest of the world* in almost everything. Not just sports. Everything. Wealth. Technology. Food supply. Educational system. Entertainment and the arts. Athletes. (Okay, maybe not chocolate and leiderhosen, but you get the idea.)

The United States especially dominated basketball. In the America of 1972, the game had an eighty-year growing history, 18 million players from all walks of life, and 150 million annual spectators.

The Soviets, on the other hand, had developed an interest in hoops, built a program, and grew it very quickly, according to noted Russian historian Yuri Brokhin in the book *Big Red Machine*, for one reason and one reason only (which, coincidentally, is the same reason they built The Bomb): "To overcome the American imperialists on land, sea and sky."

• • •

At Munich, the American team was no less dominant than in the previous seven Olympics. They had won their first seven games easily, before the terrorists struck. The horror of the tragedy put the Games on hold for two days, as the world tried to sort out the news they had heard from Jim McKay: eleven dead Israeli athletes in the Olympic Village—murdered by Palestinian terrorists.

When the Games resumed, the U.S. basketball team picked up right where it had left off, beating Italy by thirty in the semifinals.

The gold-medal game against the Soviets would go differently, though. The Americans immediately fell into the slow, deliberate pace of the Big Red Machine. "You had guys who liked to run the ball up and down the floor, and we come back on offense, you pass the ball six, seven, eight times before you can get a shot off," said U.S. guard Ed Ratleff. "That's the thing that threw us off more than anything else." His backcourt-mate Tom Henderson said, "We should have ran, and we'd have ran them back to Russia."

But the U.S.S.R. built a five-point lead at halftime with its methodical control of the game clock. The lead grew to ten with under ten minutes to play.

That's when the U.S.A. began a furious comeback, led by Kevin Joyce of South Carolina. The Americans shrunk the lead to one with thirty-eight seconds to play, but that seemed to be where the comeback came to its end. The Soviets deliberate passing game was perfect for controlling the clock and icing victory.

And with six seconds left, and the team from the U.S.S.R. beating the Americans 49-48, the players, the coaches, and the world were just starting to formulate the question in their minds: *Oh God…What does this mean?*

But then Doug Collins—the Americans' feistiest, toughest, never-say-die player out of Illinois State—intercepted a pass.

He drove to the basket. Hard.

And got fouled. Hard.

So hard, in fact, that he ended up smashed against the stanchion that holds up the goal.

Three seconds left.

Collins shook himself off. He was dazed, witless, and almost unconscious. The question became, *Would he be able to shoot these free throws? The two most important free throws in the history of international basketball?*

Assistant coaches Don Haskins and John Bach shouted to Iba: "We gotta get somebody to shoot these free throws."

But Collins heard Iba say: "If Doug can walk, he's shooting them."

That was all Collins needed to hear. He stumbled up to the line and calmly sank them both. United States 50, U.S.S.R. 49. It was the U.S.A.'s first lead of the game.

Only three seconds remained, remember, and this is the way the scoreboard was supposed to tilt—to the American side. It was the way it had always been, the way it went at the Olympics, the way it went in the way of the world. It was okay. Now nobody had to ponder what the shock of a United States powerhouse loss would mean.

You wouldn't think all hell could break loose in three tiny seconds. But you'd be wrong.

Perhaps the horn announced it—the breaking loose of all hell. During Collins' second pressure-packed free throw, the scorer's table horn had inexplicably sounded. It was a careless human mistake at best; the world's most horrifyingly inappropriate "Noonan!" at worst.

Either way, it was unfair to Collins, even though he made it a moot point for the officials by making the shot. The inadvertent horn, however, was nothing compared to what happened next.

The Soviets were taking the ball out of bounds underneath their own basket, just after Collins made his free throws. Still three seconds remaining. They were forbidden, by international rules, to call a timeout with time stopped after a free throw. They, instead, had to inbound the ball, and *then* their coach had to push a button which activated a red light, which arranged for the timeout.

This is what happened instead: Offense in chaos, ball inbounded, Soviet coach and bench spill out onto the floor demanding that the clock be stopped.

Bulgarian official Artenik Arabadjan did stop the clock with one second remaining. He ruled that fans were on the court, interrupting the game action. Problem is, the only folks on the court that *shouldn't* have been on the court were the Soviet bench players and coaches.

Arabadjan did not allow a timeout, but he did put three seconds back on the clock, and further, he allowed the Soviets another chance to inbound the ball from under their own basket.

It was a…do-over.

The Soviet player took the ball. His team ran its out-of-bounds play. He stepped on the line as he threw the ball toward half-court—a clear violation.

No call was made.

The ball hung in the air for a few seconds, and just as it came down toward the court, it was deflected by an American defender. The buzzer sounded. The game was over. Americans went wild, winners—by a narrow margin—of their eighth gold medal in a row. They kept the streak alive. Whew.

But there was an unusual stir in the crowd, an interruption of the celebration.

Come on down, R. William Jones.

At the time, Jones, hailing from Great Britain, was the secretary general of the International Amateur Basketball Federation (FIBA), and— this is important to keep in mind—he had absolutely no authority *during* an Olympic game.

There he was, though, descending from his seat in the stands. He walked directly to the scorer's table, smugly overruled the officials, granted the Soviets their timeout, and put—one more time—*three* seconds back on the clock.

It was a…do-over redux.

The Soviets lined up for their third inbounds play. The Americans matched up to defend.

Only the Brazilian referee, Renato Righetto, commanded 6-foot-11-inch Tom McMillen to back away from the inbounds passer, a rule that did not exist in international play. Righetto even threatened a technical if McMillen didn't cooperate.

So poor McMillen ended up in a position halfway between the end line and the free throw line, which was nowhere near the passer he was supposed to be guarding.

Ivan Edeshko—the passer—took full advantage of the extra space. He launched a crisp, accurate, unimpeded, length-of-the-court pass to his 6-foot-7-inch teammate Aleksandr Belov.

Belov out-leapt two American defenders (Kevin Joyce and Jim Forbes), snatched the ball out of the air, and laid it in the basket as time ran out.

The buzzer sounded.

The game was over.

The Soviets went wild, winners—by a narrow margin—of the first gold medal for any country besides the United States. It was a new streak, and a new world.

This time, there would be no do-over.

Not that the United States team didn't try. They filed a formal protest with the International Amateur Basketball Federation, with the case heard before a five-member panel the very next day. There were three communist bloc judges on the panel: a Hungarian, an Italian, and a Cuban. And it played out just like the Cold War politics of the world-at-large.

The protest was dismissed by a vote of 3-2.

But it wouldn't be the only protest.

When it came time for the medal ceremony—after the appeal was heard—the United States players took their stand. But it wasn't the silver-medal stand. They decided—as a team—that they would not accept the injustice and the untruth that was being thrust upon them. On principle, the entire team boycotted the medal ceremony, making these men the only athletes in Olympic history to have done so.

Is it fair to call this team "losers?" In the final analysis, they were more royally screwed than any other team in history. But the fact remains:

They did lose. They lost out on fairness. They lost out on the supposed "apolitical nature" of the Olympic games. They lost twelve gold medals. What they gained was the moniker, "First American basketball team to lose a game in the Olympics."

Their silver medals still—some thirty-two years later—sit in a vault in Lausanne, Switzerland, unclaimed. They're worth about $30 apiece on the silver market. They're worth absolutely nothing to the members of the 1972 U.S. Olympic Basketball Team.

13

BEFORE THE 1984 Summer Olympics in Los Angeles, Mary Decker had never run in an Olympic race. In 1972, she was too young—although probably talented enough. In 1976, she was injured. In 1980, President Carter and the United States boycotted the Games, as they were being staged in communist Moscow. Twelve years is a long, long time to wait for the one thing you desire. It's a long time to yearn for the one thing that will satisfy you. It's a long time to be at the ready, just hoping someone would say, "Go."

But the L.A. Games were Mary Decker's. She grew up in the host city. She trained just a few miles down the California coast. And she never was so ready to lean over and receive what (she believed) so rightfully belonged around her neck: an Olympic gold medal.

Decker came into those Games as the world champion in the 3,000 meters, a title she won the previous year in Helsinki. She had already easily won her semifinal heat, putting to rest any doubt in her own mind about her sore right Achilles tendon, which required a cortisone injection in July. Decker described her victory in the semis as "effortless. Except for Lynn Williams [of Canada] stepping on my heel four times." She was the kind of runner who never had to race with the pack, because she was always so far ahead of it.

In other words, she was the prohibitive favorite.

Decker's *true* main competition—world record holder Svetlana Ulmasova of the U.S.S.R.—wasn't even in L.A. (In turn for President

Carter's boycott, the Russians had withheld all competitors from the '84 Summer Games.) But Decker had other runners to worry about. Namely, Zola Budd of Great Britain and Maricica Puica of Romania. Budd was the more heralded, Puica the more dangerous.

Budd was easily recognizable—she ran barefoot. And she brought her own story with her to U.S. soil, having put herself through trauma and complications simply to get there. She left friends, school, and a pleasant, uncomplicated life on a farm in South Africa to claim British citizenship. In doing so—in running *from* apartheid-addled South Africa and running *for* good-guy Great Britain—Zola Budd created a storm of debate: "Isn't this allowing South Africa a place in international sport?" they said. "And shouldn't we *not* be doing that until they rid themselves of apartheid?"

Budd didn't want anything to do with any of that. She wished her name wasn't attached to South Africa or apartheid. She wished she could just run, free of all the controversy. She wished...she could be more like Mary Decker.

Back in her hometown of Bloemfontein, Budd kept a picture of Decker above her bed. When the two met in San Diego, just before the Olympics, she spoke of Decker: "It would be wonderful to be so pretty."

These histories meant little out on the oval track, among the competitors about to run the 3,000-meter final in the Los Angeles Coliseum. Decker and Budd saw only eight lanes, narrowed down to one after the first 150 meters. But those in the stands saw a heretofore cursed beauty finally ready to receive her due, and a timid young deer hurtling away from the storm as fast as she could.

The gun went off. And Mary Decker took off like a tennis ball from John McEnroe's racket. Smooth and relaxed, she ran at a world-record pace.

This was part of the plan. Decker's coach, Dick Brown, admitted that she was trying for "about an 8:29 pace in the final." (Ulmasova's world record was 8:26.78.) "With a kilometer to go," Brown continued, "she would begin picking it up."

Decker seemed to be trying her best to stick with the game plan, al-though, with each successive lap after the first, she lost about a second from her world-record pace. She passed the 1,600-meter mark in approxi-mately 4:35. The rest of the field crossed the same mark in…approximate-ly 4:36. Decker had shaken no one. They were a pack. And at the head of the pack was Budd, shoulder to shoulder with Decker. She had just pulled even. But she had been there from the start, just outside Decker's right shoulder. Decker knew it, could feel Budd bearing down on her. She knew it especially at 500 meters, when the two of them bumped elbows, a result of Budd's wide-swinging arm revolutions. In that moment, Decker shot Budd a sharp look.

Soon there would be "about a kilometer to go." That's when it would be time for Decker to begin to pick it up. It would be a long, ever-quick-ening drive to the finish, and it would be brutal. Decker knew that Budd would be pushing her all the way. She also knew that the rest of the pack was right behind, waiting for a mistake, or the exhaustion of the front-runner.

Budd sensed the slowing pace, sensed that Decker had been losing a precious second for every lap. And Budd didn't like it. Her natural race was one of increasing, constant pressure. On top of that, she and her coach, Pieter Labuschagne, knew that she wouldn't be able to withstand the kick of a fresh Decker or Puica. If she was to have the gold medal draped around her neck, the pace needed to be faster.

So Budd passed Decker, just after 1,600 meters, *on the turn*.

As she extended the pass all the way through the turn, she appeared to have enough margin between herself and Decker to cut into the lead posi-tion without interfering with Decker's stride. Instead, she hung wide, on the outside of lane one, going into the stretch. Budd's teammate, Wendy Sly, was now just off Budd's shoulder, and Puica cruised along in fourth, right behind Decker, waiting …

Budd began her drift to the inside. Decker sensed this, and also sensed that Budd wasn't far enough ahead to cut in. But she didn't do what any other seasoned middle-distance runner would do in this situation. She didn't reach out and touch Budd's shoulder to let her know she already had the pole position, and that there was not enough of a gap between the two of them for such a move. What Decker did do was shorten her stride.

Only for a few steps.

But enough to cause havoc.

Contact. Decker's right thigh grazed Budd's bare left foot. Budd continued along off-balance for five more strides. She tried to regain control of her body, but in the process drifted slightly to the left—toward Decker. Decker's right foot struck Budd's left calf—spiked her just above the Achilles tendon. Budd's leg shot out, and she *almost* fell.

Decker did fall. Tripped up by Budd's awkward left leg, she reached out after Budd, tore the racing number from her back, and went headlong into the infield of the track.

Decker's first thought was to get up; finish. She tried. But she couldn't. It was like she was tied to the ground. The diagnosis, which she wouldn't learn until later: a pulled gluteus, the muscle that stabilizes the hip. The result, which she knew right away: She couldn't get up.

In this moment of helplessness and uncontrol, Mary Decker fully realized her horror: She wouldn't be allowed to finish this race, this one race for which she had prepared for the past twelve years. She was denied, again, from creating her own ending to this 3,000-meter story.

The rest of the race played out before her, as medical attendants and her fiance come running across the infield.

Budd kept her feet and the lead. In fact, she increased the pace—even as the crowd booed her. Tears streamed down her face as she ran ahead of the pack in the most important race of her life, with a stadium full of people wishing against her. A thrilling moment trashed.

Perhaps the weight of it all was why Budd faded, faded, faded...all the way back to seventh place. That's where she was when she crossed the line: seventh place in 8:48.80.

Puica had plenty of energy for the last 300, and bolted away from the pack, winning in 8:35.96.

As Mary Decker and her fiance made their way across the track and into the tunnel, Budd found her. She desperately tried to make Decker—the hero whose photo hung above Budd's childhood bed—know that she had intended none of this anguish.

But Decker would have none of it. "Don't bother," she said, and waved Budd away.

In the days that followed, many people chimed in about whose fault this wrecked race was.

Fifth-place finisher Cornelia Burki of Switzerland said, "When you're behind, you're the one to have to watch out. It was Mary's fault."

Eamonn Coghlan of Ireland, the world indoor mile record-holder, stated: "You're supposed to be one stride ahead before you can cut in."

At the race, an umpire seated along the track had signaled a foul, and the referee had disqualified Budd for obstructing Decker. But in the end, a jury of appeals, after watching videotape from six different angles, saw that it was hard to place blame, and reinstated Budd.

Coghlan said it best: "Perhaps it was inexperience on Zola's part. Perhaps it was being too ladylike on Mary's part. You can't blame either one."

14

THE YEAR: 199

THE VENUE: Olympic Amphitheatre, Hamar, Norway

THE EVENT: Olympic Figure Skating Championship

ONE OF THE things that separates sports competitions from other forms of entertainment is that the athletic world doesn't have a screenwriter or director.

That seems obvious, but the implications are profound: Without a script—without someone supervising the elements to ensure a satisfactory conclusion—there's no telling what will happen. Sometimes a seemingly perfect matchup may prove crushingly boring. Sometimes the best team may lose. Sometimes...well, all the time, anything can happen.

That's not always easy to see from the distance of history—especially when history provides a near-perfect ending to a sordid story.

This one involved figure skating, an event most of us pay little attention to outside of Winter Olympic years. That's when we suddenly know the names and countries of the best in the world. That's when the finer points of camels, axels, salchows, and death spirals suddenly become important to us.

This time, even more people than usual were paying attention. And that all has to do with some key events that happened prior to the competition. A quick rundown:

January 6: Just after exiting the ice during a practice for the Olympic team trials in Detroit (where two skaters will be selected for the team), twenty-two-year-old Nancy Kerrigan is clubbed on her right knee. The attacker flees. Although U.S. Figure Skating rules state that if you don't compete, you can't be on the team, officials begin searching for a loophole to allow Kerrigan a chance to be on the team.

January 14: Derrick Smith, Shane Stant, and Shawn Eckardt are charged with assault. Eckardt—who hired the two men to arrange the attack—says that Tonya Harding, the skater he works for as a bodyguard, knew about the plan and helped with the cover-up. Harding denies it. The U.S. Olympic powers-that-be express hope that Harding—who finished first in the Olympic trials—will withdraw from the Games.

January 19: Harding's sort-of ex-husband Jeff Gillooly (they divorced, but she still refers to him as "husband") is charged with conspiracy.

January 27: Harding admits having been told of the attack...after it happened. "I had no prior knowledge of the planned assault on Nancy Kerrigan," said her prepared statement. "I am responsible, however, for failing to report things I learned about the assault when I returned home from Nationals."

February 1: Gillooly says Harding knew about the plan. He pleads guilty to a count of racketeering.

In the meantime, the U.S. Olympic Committee tried to figure out whether to let Harding compete. Yes, she had earned the spot. No, she hadn't yet been convicted—or charged—with anything. Yes, it seemed cruel and unusual for Nancy Kerrigan to have to practice on the same ice with her. No, there was no precedent anywhere in Olympic history to make such a decision.

Oh, and there was the little business of the $20 million lawsuit that Harding was dangling in front of the USOC.

Messy? You bet. And it wasn't until *after* the opening ceremonies for the Games that the committee made its ruling: Harding gets to skate if the lawsuit gets dropped. "I finally get to prove to the world I can win a gold medal," she tells the Associated Press.

• • •

This is where the story stops being about legalities—in which everything is designed for right and good to prevail—and becomes a story about athletic competition, where, as was said earlier, anything can happen.

One of the things that seemed to get lost as the mainstream press went neck and neck with the tabloids to report the scandal was that neither skater was favored to win the gold at Lillehammer. Kerrigan may have improved her act since taking a bronze in '92, but even without a banged knee, she wasn't seen as serious competition for France's Surya Bonaly or Ukraine's Oksana Baiul, the reigning world champion.

Yet when the two American skaters entered the arena to practice—repeat, *to practice*—an estimated 700 members of the media were there to witness the event. So was a security detail four times the normal size, since both parties had gotten death threats.

Kerrigan, clad in the same outfit she was wearing when she was clubbed, kept silent when her rival came out onto the ice—although she did a triple lutz in front of Harding. The two skated for a little over an hour without incident. What did the world think would happen? Harding would attack Kerrigan with a bear trap?

No, Harding was where she wanted to be. The world was watching. And she would show everyone that she could transcend the trailer-park reputation she had been saddled with by the media.

Again, a reminder: This is not a movie. This is real life. Harding could win—and perhaps become the only American Olympic champion in recent history *not* to be buried in endorsement offers or invited to tour in ice shows, unless she was asked to play the witch in *Snow White on Ice* or some other Disney extravaganza. Kerrigan could head out to the ice and have her knee give out.

Anything.

Here's what did happen.

Nancy Kerrigan—a mere fifty days after her attack, and cool as a Zamboni wheel—skated very well, nailing a triple toe loop-triple toe loop combination that led into a triple Salchow-double toe loop. Trust us, it ain't easy. The crowd went wild.

But sixteen-year-old Oksana Baiul skated better. The judges went wild.

This being a juried event and not a popularity contest, the gold went to the Ukrainian.

But Kerrigan wasn't the loser.

The loser of this story was nowhere to be found when her name was called to compete. So she was given a two-minute grace period, as is the custom.

More than a minute and a half into what would have been the most anticlimactic competition in sports history, she showed up on the ice, asthma inhaler in hand. Ditching the device, she took a moment to adjust her skate laces, then began her routine—and missed her first jump. And broke into tears. And skated to a ref and told of how her lace had broken during warm-ups. Harding was allowed to try again, after the others in her group had performed.

Good winning out? Again, this is the real world. Harding came back and hit four triple jumps, moving her from tenth place to eighth.

That's pretty good when you consider that these are the best female skaters in the world. It's not that great when most of the world no longer sees you as a plucky, pull-yourself-up-by-your-bootstraps everygal and, instead, gloats in your failure against the woman your sort-of-husband ordered clubbed.

A few more dates:

March 16: In a plea bargain, Harding pleads guilty to hindering the investigation of the attack. The deal forces her to resign from the American team competing in the world championships, turn in her membership to the U.S. Figure Skating Association, and pay penalties, undergo psychiatric evaluation, perform community service, etc.

May 31: Harding is stripped of her national championship title by the USFSA and banned for life from competition.

We could tell more...about the sex tape, about other run-ins with the law, about the once-great athlete's forays into celebrity boxing and other desperate attention-getters.

But, instead, we'll focus on the loss—a loss that wasn't preordained. Harding's boys might have gotten away with the heinous act. They might have made it possible for Harding to win an Olympic gold medal.

Sure, it wouldn't have happened in a fictional Hollywood movie.

But this is sports. Nobody knows, until the end, who the real loser is.

SEASONS ON
THE STINK

15

THE YEAR: 1962
THE VENUE: The Polo Grounds and various National League ballparks
THE EVENT: The New York Mets' first season in the big leagues

THE TICKER-TAPE parade was quite a scene. Held on lower Broadway in New York City, the event was supposed to kick off in celebratory style a new era of National League baseball in NYC. After losing the Brooklyn Dodgers and the New York Giants to California, New York now had some new kids on the block: the Mets. They were replacements for the large percentage of city dwellers who couldn't stomach the Yankee empire.

The fans wanted—no, they *needed*—the Mets. And the day before the Mets' first home game, those hungry folks flocked to that ticker-tape parade ready to buy into their new orange-and-blue-and-white-clad hometown team.

They saw the players slowly riding down the famous street, soaking in their cheers and adulation. And when the stars-of-the-day ended up on a stage with their owner, William Shea, the crowd went bonkers.

Then Mr. Shea took hold of the microphone, looked out at the excitable fans, and said…"Be patient with us until we can bring some real ballplayers in here."

Oops.

Maybe Mr. Shea set the wrong tone.

Or maybe Mr. Shea knew exactly what he was talkin' 'bout.

Because by all historical accounts, the 1962 New York Mets *weren't* real ballplayers. At least not major league-caliber ones.

Case in point: Before the season even started, pitcher Evans Killeen had…well, he had a really cool name. But he also had a really pathetic imagination. On the morning of his scheduled spring training start, Killeen had somehow managed to slice his thumb while shaving. He told manager Casey Stengel the situation and, of course, Stengel asked him what he was doing shaving his thumb.

Killeen's answer?

He couldn't come up with one.

At which point he got the ax—Stengel sent him home. Yes, Evans Killeen was cut from the lousiest team in baseball history. (The phrase "worse than bad," if you really consider it, doesn't seem sensible. Like "beating a dead horse," it's redundant. However, in this case, getting cut from such an awful team does, in fact, make Evans Killeen *worse than bad*.)

Another case in point: The first run the Mets ever scored came not on an RBI single or a home run or a double off the wall. Hell, it didn't even come from a walked batsman that forced in a run (which would have been embarrassing enough). No, the Mets' first run of their first game of their first season came in the third inning, when St. Louis Cardinals pitcher Larry Jackson balked with Mets slugger Richie Ashburn on third base. Yes, Ashburn was balked home, which is a lot like winning a point in a tennis match because your opponent kept hitting into the net.

And another case in point: After opening their season on Friday the 13th of April, the Mets promptly lost their first nine games. Somehow—defying logic and reason—they found themselves 9½ games out of first place. How is that even possible, you ask? Well, the Pittsburgh Pirates started 10-0, and on the same day, the Mets were 0-9, so there were nine full games' difference, plus the extra one the Pirates had already won and the Mets hadn't yet played, which counts for a half-game in the standings. To be more games out of first place than you've even played is…again, *worse than bad*.

And another: Ashburn played center field for this cast of castoffs, and he was frightfully out of place. A Hall of Famer in the twilight of his career, he could still hit and field, and he played the game with pride. One day, Ashburn pulled aside Elio Chacon, the Mets young shortstop who kept screwing up defensively on popups to short center field. Ashburn told Chacon that outfielders calling loudly for a fly ball have the right of way over back-pedaling infielders. Unfortunately, Chacon did not understand, since his grasp of the English language was less than adequate. Luckily, though, a bilingual teammate shared with Ashburn that the correct phrase to alert Chacon to get out of the way was, "Yo la tengo!"

The next time a popup was lifted out to short center, Ashburn had a bead on it. In a full sprint, he began yelling, "Yo la tengo! Yo la tengo!" Chacon—message received—immediately pulled out of the way. Which is when Ashburn was bowled over by charging leftfielder Frank Thomas.

And yet another: The staff ace on the '62 Mets was Roger Craig. His record? 10-*24*. Al Jackson, the number two man, was 8-20. That's right: Two twenty-game losers, which is almost unheard of. But the Mets did one better: Jay Hook went 8-19 (ooh, so close). And then they did one better than that: Craig Anderson won 3 and lost 17. Four guys with over 17 losses. That's amazing. (Hey, maybe that's how they got their nickname?)

And one more: "Marvelous" Marv Throneberry. Period. To those who had the fortune and pleasure of seeing Marvelous Marv play first base, he was a cult figure, an icon, a legend. His very-ordinary career stats (.237 average and fifty-three homers in seven major league seasons) belie how marvelously wretched he was as a player. In one game, Al Jackson pitched fifteen innings and gave up only three hits, but the Mets lost the game on two errors by Marvelous. (Rumor has it that it was in the wake of this particular game that Casey Stengel frustratedly belted out his famous line, "Can't anybody here play this game?")

Still, as bad as those game-killing errors were, there was no greater thrill for Throneberry-followers than the June day Marvelous Marv cost New York *six* runs in one inning against the Cubs. In the top half of the first, he bumped into a Chicago baserunner during a rundown, allowing one run to score and—in the final tally—three more to follow. Then—and this is even better—Throneberry came up to bat in the bottom half of the inning. He proceeded to rip a rare triple with two outs, which, for an instant, scored two runners. Except that Marvelous was called out for having missed the bag when he rounded second base. The runs did not count, of course.

Casey Stengel came out of the dugout to argue, but the umpire stopped him short: "Uh, Case, I wouldn't argue this one too much. He missed first base, too."

There's more: With the first pick in the expansion draft, the Mets made journeyman catcher Hobie Landrith their first pick. Stengel, with a distinct lack of excitement, said: "You gotta have a catcher. If you don't have a catcher, you'd have all passed balls." Unfortunately, Landrith wasn't out on the field enough to stop many of the pitches. The Mets used seven different catchers in '62, none of whom had more than 158 at-bats.

How 'bout this one? (Keep in mind, the following all occurred in a single inning of a game in Cincinnati in August.)

With one out in the third, and runners on first and third, pitcher Al Jackson gets the Reds hitter to hit a grounder to Throneberry at first. Marvelous throws—belatedly—to home plate, when, in fact, the 3-6-3 double play, or the 3-unassisted-6 double play would have been the options of choice (and would have gotten the Mets out of the inning). Okay, one run scored, but there are still Reds on first and second with one out— another good double-play situation.

Jackson walks a man. No harm done. Now there's a force at any base, and still the chance for the inning-ending doubleplay.

Ground ball, hit right at second baseman Ron Kanehl. Perfect. Or not. Kanehl misplays it off his leg and leaves the bases still loaded with one out.

On Jackson's next pitch, all the Reds' runners break. Another grounder to Kanehl. This time, he fields it smoothly and flips it to second to start the double play. Problem is, the Reds' runner from first is already standing on the bag. Another run scores.

Yet Jackson is unflappable. He forces another Red to hit a ground ball, this time to shortstop Charley Neal. Long-time New York baseball scribe Jimmy Breslin describes Neal's ensuing play in his book, *Can't Anybody Here Play This Game?*: "The temptation was to go for the inning-ending double play, short-to-second-to-first. It looked easy. But you were not going to get Charley Neal into a sucker game like this. No, sir. Charley straightened up and fired the ball to first to get one out. The fourth run of the inning came across."

Four double play balls. Four Reds runs. That's a special form of perfection...

Here's another one for you: Manager Stengel, "The Old Perfessor," told his Mets outfielders: "When one of them guys hits a single to you, throw the ball to third. That way we can hold them to a double."

And another: The Mets hit .240 as a team, good for last in the majors.

And another: New York's pitching staff ERA stuck at 5.04, a half-run worse than any other team.

And another: 210 errors. Meanwhile, no other team had more than 173.

And yet another: Losing streaks of seventeen, thirteen, and eleven games.

Still another: 60½ games out of first. (Eighteen games behind the next-to-last place Cubs; twenty-four behind fellow expansion team the Houston Colt .45s.)

Look, we could point to all the different reasons why the 1962 Mets, with their 40-120 record, were the worst team in baseball history. But numbers don't tell the story. They don't get it to sink in. Seeing Marvelous Marv Throneberry run the bases...that would've done the job. Watching Rod Kanehl boot one off his foot...that, too, would've worked. Observing Craig Anderson lose seventeen games as a reliever would impress the idea upon you, as well.

Or you could just know how the very last play of the Mets' horrendous inaugural season went: Trailing the Cubs, 5-1, the Mets started a rally. Sammy Drake and Richie Ashburn singled. Two on, no outs, with Joe Pignatano up to bat. Pignatano hit a soft liner in the direction of Cubs second baseman Ken Hubbs. Hubbs caught it, looked around and realized that both Drake and Ashburn were way too far off their respective bags. Apparently, they assumed Hubbs couldn't get to it. So...Hubbs threw to second base, the shortstop tossed it over to first, and, on a seldom-seen triple play, the season was over.

Who's the best? *Not* the Mets, Mets, Mets.

16

THE YEAR: 1972-'73
THE VENUE: Philadelphia's Spectrum and various NBA arenas
THE EVENT: The 76ers' season

ONE OF THE greatest arguments in sports is the MVP argument, and it goes a little something like this:

On the one side, you've got the folks who only want to know: who is the best player in the league? That's it. That's your answer. When you find him, you've found your MVP. No matter how good or bad his team is.

On the other side, the criteria is a bit different: which guy, if taken off his team, would cause his team to absolutely crumble? This side believes you must take into account the team's position in the standings. If said team is horrendous, then its best player isn't all that valuable.

What makes this one of the greatest arguments in sports is two things: (1) It's renewed, among fans and writers and players and coaches, every year; (2) It isn't limited to a particular sport.

So whose side are we on?

The latter group. Why? They're the people who believe there's a reason why it's MVP and not MOP (Most Outstanding Player). That V stands for Valuable, and to figure out who that is, they've got to go a little below the surface.

And for all their efforts, we'd like to present them with this treasure of a should-have-been-MVP example: Billy Cunningham.

Any good argument needs background info, and here's ours: In 1970-'71, the Philadelphia 76ers went 47-35, good for second in the NBA's newly formed Atlantic Division. Clearly, the team's best player was Cunningham.

He averaged 23.0 points per game. He led the team in rebounding, with nearly twelve per contest. And he was second on the team in assists, with a 4.9 average. Cunningham improved on all three categories in the play-offs, pushing his rebounds up over fifteen per game, his assists up to almost six, and his scoring up to 25.7.

The following year, the Sixers traded guard Archie Clark to Baltimore for Kevin Loughery and Fred Carter. They also obtained Bob Rule and Bill Bridges in trades. With all the new faces on this team in transition, the record suffered at 30-52. But the future looked bright, especially with Billy Cunningham still shining brightly, leading the way. He averaged 5.9 assists, 12.2 rebounds, and 23.3 points per game, and carried the team on his shoulders to many of its wins.

This is where you will start to see how this situation is so appropriate to the argument: Billy Cunningham abruptly left the 76ers after the 1971-'72 season to join the ABA's Carolina Cougars, and whatever part of the dam he had been holding together was suddenly a leaky—no, gushing—mess.

The 1972-'73 Sixers—sans Cunningham—were a disaster.

The bad stuff was in full effect when a new coach arrived in town: Roy Rubin, who had no previous NBA experience (although he spent eleven successful years at Division I University of Rhode Island). "It was a joke, like letting a teenager run a big corporation," team leader Fred Carter told *Sports Illustrated* some years later. The biggest complaints against Rubin were that he was in over his head; he wasn't familiar with the NBA style, nor did he know the players around the league. "We had [Hall of Fame guard] Hal Greer on that team, and Rubin had no idea who he was. After we went 4-4 in the preseason, Rubin said, 'I don't think Boston will be so tough.' We just looked at each other and laughed," Carter said.

Rubin's Sixers lost their first fifteen games, and put themselves into a bigger hole than the Grand Canyon. From those First Fifteen, "it was clear we were the league's universal health spa," Carter explained. "If teams had any ills, they got healthy when they played us."

As you might be able to gather, the team didn't have much respect for Roy Rubin. Still, what John Q. Trapp did on December 20 was *way* over the line. In a 141-113 blowout loss, Rubin was trying to keep his troops fresh as they were run up, down, around and over by the Pistons. But when he sent a substitute in for Trapp, John Q. refused to come out of the game. He, apparently, wanted his garbage-time minutes. Badly. When Rubin insisted that the forward heed his instructions, Trapp told the coach to look behind the Sixers' bench. There, the legend goes, one of Trapp's consorts opened his jacket to reveal a handgun. Rubin gulped, turned back to the court, and left John Q. Trapp in for the rest of the game. No use getting killed just to hold a team under 140 points.

Besides that Pistons scoring orgy, the 76ers gave up 130 points in twelve games during that 1972-'73 season, and 120 points in a mind-blowing *thirty-four* games. Along with their fifteen-game opening-season streak, Philly had a fourteen-game losing steak in December and January, then topped those both with a twenty-gamer. They even finished the season by losing their last thirteen games. (Who knows how long that would've lasted had the season not mercifully ended.)

At the All-Star break, Philly got rid of Rubin. They named Kevin Loughery player-coach, and one of his first orders of business was to re-lease John Q. Trapp. Which didn't change things too much—except for the coach's on-court safety level.

Still, the city of Philadelphia watched while its team struggled almost as much without Rubin as it did with him.

It couldn't have happened to a more impatient bunch of fans. Philly sports boosters are known for their "What have you done for me in the last thirty seconds?" attitudes. They boo without much provocation; they curse with even less. They seem to wait for that moment—when one thing goes wrong, before they even know how bad it could possibly get—and pounce on it with all their emotion and anger and bitching and moaning.

Maybe it's not all bad that these are the people who had to sit through an entire season that had the rival Celtics finishing *fifty-nine* games ahead of them in the standings. There were very few moments for them to boo and curse because the whole season was one big, long f-bomb.

Somehow, in February, the Sixers reeled off five wins in seven games. It's hard to come up with an explanation for it, so let's just move on.

Because immediately following that five-of-seven streak came the thirteen losses to run out the year.

Sooooo fitting.

Fred Carter was the only real highlight from the Sixers team. He led them in almost every important category (except rebounds), mainly because...well, somebody has to shoot, pass and dribble up the court when a team gets the ball in its hands. Apparently, the rest of the Sixers were willing to let Carter do all of it.

Rubin's coaching career was forever ruined by the awful '72-'73 season, so he did about the best thing he could: Moved to Florida and bought an International House of Pancakes franchise. Seems to have developed a good attitude about the whole thing, too: "I don't hold any grudges," he told *SI*, "but the day I came in, Billy Cunningham—the team's best player—jumped to the ABA. Things went downhill from there."

And there's the real story. Billy Cunningham was so important—so Valuable—to his franchise, that when he left, the rest of the players recessed into the Worst Team in the History of the NBA.

What a terrible title.

But what a great case for Billy Cunningham as one of the most—if not *the most*—valuable players of all time.

17

THE YEAR: 1976
THE VENUE: Tampa Stadium
THE EVENT: The Buccaneers' first NFL season

THE ST. PETERSBURG Times said it best: For an entire NFL season (1976-
'77), the Tampa Bay Bucs had "an unrelenting vendetta against victory."

0-14.

Oh-and-fourteen.

Guess how many other teams in NFL history have failed to win a
single game. Go ahead, guess.

If you said, "None," or, "Zero," you'd be right. But as with any grim—er,
great—story, the numbers just hint at the story.

Let's start minutes before the season even started, as the Bucs were
finishing up their pre-game warm-ups for its first-ever contest in franchise history. Coach John McKay intended to take his team back to the
locker room for some last-minute encouragement and strategy.

Good intentions. Bad execution. Because forty-five players, eight
coaches, a gaggle of team doctors, trainers and equipment men, and one
very grumpy old coach couldn't find their way through the Astrodome.
They toured the concrete bowels of the stadium like Spinal Tap searching for the stage, until a security guard found them and led them to the
locker room. The team made it out to the field with just minutes to go
before kickoff.

Could they blame the ensuing 20-0 loss—with only 108 yards of total
offense—on the shortened prep time?

Perhaps. Except how would that explain why, in the next game—when they found their locker room without any problem—their thirty-nine offensive plays netted *negative* yardage?

And how would it begin to explain why the team didn't score a touchdown until its fourth game?

And why, when they finally did, it was defensive: a 44-yard fumble recovery returned for the score.

"They were absolutely horrible, and that's the nicest thing I can say about them," said not an irate fan, not a cynical newspaper columnist, but the team's coach, after the team racked up its eighth straight loss. (By the way, you know you're doing poorly if your coach uses the word "they" instead of "us.")

"They" allowed the New York Jets its first shutout in thirteen seasons (one of Tampa Bay's four scoreless games that season). "Their" defense spent more than ninety plays per game on the field (compared to an average defense's thirty to fifty plays).

Okay, so nobody really expects a brand new team to vanquish many foes. What about the Bucs' match-up with 1976's other expansion team, the Seattle Seahawks?

That duel, the Expansion Bowl, happened during Week Five, in Tampa. Both teams were winless going into their game, so chances were, somebody would be leaving with their first win (whether they deserved it or not.) Turned out, neither team really deserved it. But the game was close, and in the end, Tampa Bay's *thirty* penalties did them in. Final score: Seahawks 13, Bucs 10.

Yes, we said *thirty* penalties.

From that point on, the Tampa fans stopped rooting for wins and started rooting for their place in history.

"Go for 0."

Hey, at least they were still rooting.

Perhaps the best instance of fan loyalty came at the end of Thanksgiving weekend (or, Week Twelve). The Bucs flew out to Oakland to face the Super Bowl-bound Raiders. The game was ugly—a 49-16 pasting—but the plane ride was worse: six hours aboard a horribly vibrating old Boeing 707 that the team borrowed from the McCullough chainsaw company president, a close friend of Coach McKay's.

By the time Air McCullough arrived in Tampa, it was 4 a.m. The plane taxied to its usual spot at the airport, rolled up to the stairs, and opened its doors.

That's when the team heard...it.

"What have we got?"

"Bucs Fever!"

"What have we got?"

"Bucs Fever!"

"What have we got?!"

"BUCS FEVER!"

Three members of the Bucs Booster Club stood at the foot of the stairs on the runway. One guy was leading the cheer; the other two were shouting their reply while holding up a huge, orange Bucs banner. All three were obscenely drunk.

And as, one by one, the Bucs team descended the stairs from their rattletrap of a 707, the three unwavering (in their support for the team, not in their ability to stand up straight) fans continued their chant: "What have we got?"

"BUCS FEVER!"

The nightmare season continued in Denver, where McKay was geared up for a win against the Broncos, coached by John Ralston, an old rival of McKay's from their Pac-8 days.

As the third quarter in the Mile High City rolled around, shockingly, the Bucs were still in it. In fact, they were winning—13-10. (They should have been up, 17-10, on an interception return for a touchdown by linebacker Calvin Peterson. Unfortunately, Peterson never made it to the promised land. He snagged the ball, broke away from the pack with nothing but wide-open grass in front of him...and his bum knee buckled. Untouched, he fell down on the spot, and his team had to settle for a field goal. Why was no one surprised?)

Still, the Bucs were ahead.

But not for long. Haven Moses scored for the Broncos on a 71-yard pass. Randy Gradishar intercepted a pass and found his way into the end zone. Doug Williams was sacked and fumbled deep in his own Bucs territory, and two plays later, the Broncos scored again. Then there was another interception returned for a TD. Finally, another fumble picked up by Denver, followed by a lateral, followed by a touchdown. All told: thirty-eight unanswered points in a little more than a quarter. Final score (and remember, the game was 13-10, Bucs, late in the third): 48-13, Broncos.

Go for 0. Fine. But do you have to go *so* hard?

Up to this point, Coach McKay had been fairly patient with the losing. But here's where he snapped. In his postgame press conference, McKay, upset over a fourth-quarter reverse and believing Denver offensive coordinator Max Corley was trying to run up the score on his overmatched team, called him a—well, we'll let McKay say it: "He was a prick when I knew him at Oregon, he's a prick now and he'll always be a prick."

The matter got even messier when *Time* magazine mistakenly reported that McKay had called *Ralston* that unpleasantry. Wanna dig a little deeper, Coach? "I would have called him a prick," McKay told a Tampa writer, "but a prick has a head."

And on and on and on to season's end, when players couldn't get away fast enough. Defensive end Pat Toomay noted that after the final, 31-14, loss to the New England Patriots, the players' parking lot, filled with U-Hauls, station wagons, pickup trucks, and overstuffed luggage racks *before* the last game, "looked like the staging area for a bunch of Okies fleeing the Dust Bowl."

The players were embarrassed, discouraged, and beaten down. But the coach...

When John McKay took the job in Tampa (after many years of success on the collegiate level at USC), he had announced that he could coach the NFL from his armchair watching it on TV.

A year in the league had proved him wrong. Way, way, *way* wrong.

And, in the wake of the humiliation, on *his* way out of town, McKay was singing a different tune.

"I'll probably take some time off," McKay said, "and go hide someplace."

18

THE YEAR: 1993
THE VENUE: NHL arenas
THE EVENT: The Ottawa Senators' and the San Jose Sharks' battle for the number-one pick in the entry draft

ON FEBRUARY 10, 1993, the San Jose Sharks took an early 1-0 lead over the Calgary Flames. Then they lapsed briefly, and allowed thirteen unanswered goals.

Okay, so maybe the lapse wasn't so brief, and it was much worse than we should expect from a professional sports franchise.

For the Sharks, it was the most embarrassing loss in the two-year history of the franchise. That's saying something, considering San Jose had won only seventeen games in 1991-'92, and was on its way to setting a record no team wants: fewest wins in a season. In hockey, that record was held by the 1974-'75 Washington Capitals (six measly wins), who were themselves an expansion team.

It's understandable for an expansion team to fight with such futility; it works that way in almost every sport. Because expansion teams choose players that the other teams are willing to let go—exchangeable journeyman parts, you might call them. The expansioneers end up with no star power, inexperienced youngsters getting major playing time, an extremely weak bench, and tons of attitude and work ethic problems. Such teams' first years are often riddled with lack of on-ice (or on-field or on-court) chemistry and cohesion, stretches of total offensive and defensive ineptitude, and long losing streaks.

So, had the Sharks been an expansion team, their near-record futility would have been easier to swallow. Their thirteen-goals-allowed against Calgary would have been more excusable. But the Sharks weren't in an expansion year. They should have had some cohesion; their young players should have been gaining confidence; they should have been able to stop the bleeding of long losing streaks or defensive lapses.

But...thirteen goals they gave up. *Thirteen.* An NFL team would have to score two touchdowns to get there, and that's counting by sixes. Eight Flames finished with at least two points in that game: Theoren Fleury was plus-nine; and even the goaltender—the freakin' goaltender!—Jeff Reese got into the multi-score column, setting a record for points by a netminder in a single game with his three assists.

Unfortunately, that 13-1 loss followed a pattern: It was the sixteenth of what would become a league-record-tying seventeen consecutive losses. Which, unfortunately, also followed a pattern: The seventeen-game losing streak was predated by nine- and thirteen-game losing streaks earlier in the season.

San Jose? Try Sad Jose.

But there was some good news: The Sharks weren't the only lousy team in the NHL in 1993.

The sad-sack Ottawa Senators were neck-and-neck with Sad Jose for the-opposite-of-bragging rights. (On second thought, maybe that wasn't such good news. It's actually an awful lot like, "Yeah, okay. You caught me having sex with an intern in the Oval Office...but Kennedy had a lot of sex in there, too.")

The 1992-'93 Senators were an expansion team, so that squad had an excuse to fall back on. But even it couldn't explain away how precisely poor the Ottawans were. After beating the eventual Stanley Cup champion Montreal Canadiens, 5-3, in their first game of the year, the Sens won only one game away from their home ice. (For those scoring at home, that road record was one-and-the-season. The "one" didn't happen until mid-April, and it was the Senators' only victory overall in the last six weeks of the season.)

The Senators' awful '92-'93 season was complete and utter—by that, we mean that its horrid-ness lasted from game one to game eighty-four.

Along the way, there was a twenty-one-game winless streak (0-20-1) in October and November and a fourteen-game losing streak extending throughout the entire month of March. There was the 12-3 blowout versus Buffalo right at the apex (or, rather, nadir) of the October-November freefall. There were the Los Angeles Kings' twenty-five shots on goal in *the second period* of a January game.

The Ottawa Senators were so bad that their hometown newspaper, *The Citizen*, monitored their progress with a regular box headlined "Capital Punishment." It was an homage to that long-ago Washington Capitals team that finished with just 21 points. The Senators weren't too far off track, with their twenty-six consecutive road losses.

And the Sharks were right there with them, with an 8-55-2 mark on March 8.

But things really heated up as the season wore down.

Because these two Titans of Terrible Hockey—the San Jose Sharks and the Ottawa Senators—were competing for something. Something big. As each team lost and lost and lost some more, they began to see the light at the end of the tunnel: the first pick in next year's draft. That number-one-pick was—and is—always looked at as the pot of gold, the savior, the one-way ticket out of the lowest level of Hades. And in hockey—where there was no lottery—the worst team always got him.

In 1993, the pot of gold's name was Alexandre Daigle, a 6-foot left-handed center from Montreal. He was a perfect fit for the Sharks because he had a Mario Lemieux-like combination of blazing skate speed, soft scoring touch around the net, and a strong upper body. He was also handsome, charismatic, and obliging with media and fans. But he was an even more perfect fit for the Senators because he was bilingual, crucial to a team with a 30-percent francophone target audience.

So the race was on: Who would be the worst team in hockey in 1993, with an outside chance at becoming the worst team in hockey history? Who would win the Daigle Cup?

Both teams sunk to pretty low depths.

The Sharks fished for positives, and came up with decomposing tires: Public relations director Tim Bryant liked to point out that Arturs Irbe had the first shutout in franchise history, and that Rob Gadreau had the first and second hat tricks. But then Bryant got to the real truth: "Of course, we did lose both those games." And at the end of the seventeen-game losing streak, the only highlight captain Doug Wilson could come up with was: "The resiliency the guys showed during our seventeen-game losing streak. When things got bad, I've seen guys go into a survival mode, blaming teammates instead of looking in the mirror. It never happened here." (Which is a little like saying, "Yes, I was forced to eat dog food, three meals a day, seventeen days straight. But, hey, I never had an empty stomach.")

The Senators did more than fish for positives—they tried to create one to cover up the fact that with a week left in February, they still hadn't scored enough points to pass the Capitals and keep their names out of the history books. Ottawa management proposed that the two losers agree that whichever club finished with the most points would be rewarded with the first pick in the June draft. In the words of one *Citizen* columnist, it was a way to "turn the turtle derby into a horse race."

And, to be fair, it wasn't a bad idea. Because what happened in that 1992-'93 hockey season is what happens a lot in all major professional sports: The management of the worst teams start to allow...not mind... become friends with...hope for...wish for...losses. They crave losses. Because losses will bring the number-one pick. Losses—in 1993—would win the Daigle Cup.

Both hockey teams piled up enough losses to come close to satisfying the cravings. Going into the last game of the season, the Sens had only ten wins (with four ties), and the Sharks had eleven wins (with two ties). Had the Senators won their last game against the Boston Bruins, they would have pulled ahead of the Sharks in the standings, and cost themselves Alexandre Daigle.

But Ottawa did not have to worry about it, because they lost to the Bruins, 4-2. They "won" the Daigle Cup. They assured themselves 24 meager points—three more than the lowly Caps, whose names remained in the record books.

The Sharks also ended with 24 meager points, but since their win-column total was one more than the Senators', they lost out on that first draft pick.

Senators management couldn't have been happier—to be out of the record books and in position to obtain Daigle. Owner Bruce Firestone remarked on February 28, the night his team beat Quebec to move past the Capitals: "There will only be two teams who'll achieve all their goals at the end of the season: the Ottawa Senators and the winner of the Stanley Cup."

And he was right.

And sure enough, at the end of the season, allegations surfaced.

Apparently, once the Senators' had their proposal turned down by the Sharks, they decided they *must have* that number-one pick, so…they plotted ways to assure that final loss to Boston. Firestone admitted to *Ottawa Citizen* columnist Roy MacGregor that the Senators were prepared to pull their goalie against the Bruins, which would have left an open net and bunch of weak Ottawa defensemen to stop the powerful Boston offense. Firestone also said that he had guaranteed four players roster spots for the next season if they helped assure the Bruins loss. "It is no coincidence," Firestone confided in MacGregor, "that those four players will be back with the team next season." He also added that he had a hard time "keeping the restraints" on his coach, Rick Bowness, during the final weeks of the season.

When asked to defend himself against the allegations, Firestone said: "We're all human beings. To say that the importance of drafting first had not entered my mind is untrue. But you think about these things, and you reject improper behavior. What was important is that like all people of integrity, we decided not to do it."

And he was right; the game bore that out. The Senators never pulled their goalie. Never needed to. They were bad enough to lose without helping themselves do it.

Of course, the real losers for the season were the Sad Jose Sharks. They were literally just as awful as the Senators, but they didn't get the door prize at the end. The Sharks were left with the sixth pick in the draft, who turned out to be Victor Kozlov, who wasn't nearly as sexy as Alexandre Daigle.

A funny thing happened, though, and it presents a truth about desperate losers—a truth that gets compounded when they do it unethically: The losing follows them around.

See, the Ottawa Senators did draft Alexandre Daigle with the first pick in the 1993 draft, and he played with the team for the better part of five seasons. But Daigle never turned out to be the pot of gold they had hoped, the savior of the franchise who could immediately right the ship. He wasn't even the best rookie on his own team. (That honor belonged to Alexei Yashin.) His $12.5 million contract handcuffed Ottawa, and the rookie center helped increase the team's win total to a whopping fourteen.

No, Alexandre Daigle ended up being "The Franchise" that never was, a decent scorer on a (to put it kindly) less-than-decent team. And that team had to wait five years to even sniff a winning record.

CHOKE HOLDERS

19

THE YEAR: 1964
THE VENUES: Philadelphia's Connie Mack Stadium, St. Louis' Busch Stadium, and Cincinnati's Crosley Field
THE EVENT: The National League pennant race

GUS TRIANDOS platooned at catcher for the Philadelphia Phillies. He wasn't a great player, but then, neither were most of the 1964 Phillies. Of the relevant names, only Bunning, Callison, and Allen would be remembered long into history. None of these Phillies would make the Hall of Fame.

What they were was a good team having a great year. To a man, they contributed, forming a cohesive unit and picking each other up when one hit a slump. And like the platooner Triandos told Larry Merchant of the *Philadelphia Daily News*: "This is the Year of the Blue Snow." What he meant was that it was a rare year, one where whatever happened, things seemed to work out for the best.

Things had been going so good, in fact, that in mid-September the organization announced World Series ticket prices for a four-game package: $9 for a bleacher seat, $17 for a reserved seat, and $25 to sit in a box.

As soon as the sale was announced, the championship-starved city went nuts. More than 60,000 World Series ticket applications had been received by the team, with only 20,000 accepted. (The other 15,000 were for season-ticket holders, the media, players' families and the commissioner's office.) Phillie Fever was so wild that a group of 2,000 loyalists—including Mayor James Tate—had gathered at Philadelphia International Airport in the wee morning hours to welcome their heroes back from the West Coast.

The previous day, ace right-hander Jim Bunning (eighteen wins, fivelosses) halted a two-game losing streak by pitching the Phils to a 3-2 victory in Los Angeles over the Dodgers. As it stood on September 21, the Phillies were 6½ games ahead of the Cardinals and Reds with only twelve remaining. That night would be the first game of a seven-game homestand—three with the Reds and four with the Milwaukee Braves. If the Phillies won four of these seven, it would be almost impossible for either Cincinnati or St. Louis to catch up. Strike that. It was almost impossible for them to catch up now.

The Phillies, if not a spectacular collection of talent, certainly had key components. They had an ace pitcher in Bunning. They had a bona fide star in right fielder Johnny Callison, whose three-run homer won the All-Star Game that year. And they had the best rookie in the game, third baseman Richie Allen, who was on his way to twenty-nine homers and ninety-one RBIs for the season. More important than these components, though, was the brightest young manager in baseball: Gene Mauch. He was the 1962 NL Manager of the Year. He had brought this team from 107 losses only three years earlier to the brink of the pennant. Mauch was a daring tactician, a brilliant strategist, and a powerful motivator who spoke the young players' language. He was not taking this pennant-clinching for granted. He was a nervous man. And he was warning anyone who would listen—mostly, his team: "Just remember, the 1950 Phillies had a 7½ game lead with only eleven games to play. But they lost eight of their next ten and had to win the last game to save the pennant."

Mauch had a bad premonition of how the season would play out on Saturday night in L.A. The game with the Dodgers had lasted into the sixteenth inning. Both teams had used up most of their relief pitchers. With two outs in the bottom of inning sixteen, Willie Davis singled off Phillies pitcher Jack Baldschun. The speedy Davis stole second and took third on a wild pitch by Baldschun. Mauch was forced to bring in rookie lefthander Morrie Steevens, who had just joined the team in L.A. after being called up from Little Rock. This was a tough spot for the kid. Two outs, bottom of the sixteenth, man on third, first major league appearance. What happened? In the middle of the rookie's windup, Davis broke for home. He *stole home*. With two outs. In extra innings. To win the game.

To start this series with the Reds at Connie Mack Stadium in Philly, Mauch chose Art Mahaffey. It turned out to be the right choice. He and John Tsitouris—the Reds' pitcher who had a rep as a Phillie nemesis—pitched a scoreless duel into the sixth. Suddenly, the Reds bats came alive. Chico Ruiz singled to right. Vada Pinson ripped a line drive off Mahaffey's glove and into right field, and when he tried to advance his single into a double, Phillie right fielder Johnny Callison nailed him at second. But Ruiz advanced to third. This brought Frank Robinson to the plate. Robinson was pure power. He was going to be swinging away. And on Mahaffey's first pitch, he whiffed from the heels.

On the next pitch, Ruiz took off for home.

The guy must have been crazy, because Robinson had no idea he was coming. If he took another from-the-heels swing...goodnight Ruiz. Luckily for Ruiz, the ball was way outside. Robinson didn't take the bat off his shoulder, catcher Clay Dalrymple leapt to grab the ball, and Ruiz scored standing up. Un-luckily for the Phillies, they had just lost their second game in a row by allowing the opposing team to steal home, because Tsitouris threw his first shutout of the season.

Seriously: Two games in a row? Had this ever happened before? This was definitely not a good omen. Mauch's stomach must have been a knot.

The Phillies' lead was down to 5½.

The next night, Tuesday, the Phillies got walloped by the Reds, 9-2. Meanwhile, the Cardinals won a squeaker against the league-doormat Mets.

That 5½–game lead was now 4½. The Cards were right there, too, just a half-game behind the Reds. Cardinals manager Johnny Keane pointed out: "The Phillies are slipping a little and that gives us a chance. We play them three more times, all at home. Then they must play their last two in Cincinnati. They're not in yet."

You said it. The Phillies lost *again* to the Reds, 6-4, to complete the clean sweep. Now all those folks who had gone to the trouble of completing a World Series ticket application were beginning to wonder if they should submit it. And the pain didn't stop. Thursday, the Phils lost to the Milwaukee Braves and their starter, Wade Blasingame, a twenty-year-old rookie up from the Braves minor league affiliate in Denver.

Base-running blunders played a big part in this loss. In the sixth inning, Richie Allen, running from first to second, tried to break up a double play. He overslid the bag. What he didn't realize was that Blasingame's throw had pulled shortstop Sandy Alomar off second base. Alomar tagged Allen out. Then, the very next batter, Vic Power, bounced a ball to third baseman Eddie Mathews. Mathews bobbled the ball, and Power was safe. But Alex Johnson—who had reached base on the Alomar tag play—took a wide turn after advancing to second. Mathews' throw beat the diving Johnson back to second. Inning over. Threat overcome. Phillies lose.

What was once a promise of rare blue snow was turning into an inability to avoid yellow snow.

And we all know what happened from there.

On Thursday, the Cardinals took both games of a twi-night doubleheader from Pittsburgh, and sat only 3½ games behind the Phillies. On Friday, the Cards won again, and so did the Reds. Of course, the Phillies lost to the Braves, dragging their once-mighty lead down to 1½ games over Cincinnati and 2½ over St. Louis. But the agony didn't end there.

The next day, Saturday, Philadelphia lost again. This time, it was a managerial decision by Mauch that pushed the loss button. When the Braves loaded the bases in the eighth, lefty Ed Bailey walked to the batter's box to pinch hit. Mauch elected to lift his pitcher for lefthander Bobby Shantz, a better matchup. Bench coach Harry (Peanuts) Lowrey asked, "Do you want to get Dalrymple in the game?" Everyone knew Dalrymple was a better defensive catcher than Triandos.

But Mauch decided, "No. My daughter could catch Shantz." Which might have been true, but Triandos didn't fare as well. Shantz's fourth pitch skidded off the catcher's mitt for a passed ball. This was when Mauch started talking to himself in a low mumble.

The Phillies ended up losing their sixth straight game and their ninth of their last eleven. Their lead stood at a teeny-weeny half-game over the Reds.

The next day, in a desperation move, Mauch chose his ace, Bunning, to start on two days' rest. Even this backfired. The dependable eighteen-game winner got shellacked for ten hits and seven runs in only three innings and the Phils lost in a rout, 14-8. The Reds, meanwhile, won another doubleheader in New York against the Mets, and suddenly found themselves in first place by a full game. And the Cardinals, riding a five-game winning streak, were only one-half game back of the Phillies.

What was once to be the glorious culmination of a long, hard-fought, victorious season for the Philadelphia Phillies and their fans—this seven-game homestand—had turned into an absolute nightmare. "The blackest seven days in Philadelphia baseball history," *Inquirer* columnist Allen Lewis branded it. Philadelphia fans are known to have little patience with their teams; they are considered the most brutal, unforgiving, turn-on-you-in-a-heartbeat rooters out there. And during that last game, they rained boos down. The whole team got some.

The Phillies had to be glad to be out of the heat of their hometown. But it didn't do much to relax them with a three-game series in St. Louis with the red-hot Cardinals looming. And everyone could sense the sinking ship that was the Philadelphia Phillies.

Mauch tried to present a positive front by comparing this pennant race to a round of golf. "You bogey the first hole, and everybody says, 'You just got off to a bad start.' You bogey the eleventh hole, in the month of July, say, and nobody says anything. You bogey the seventeenth hole and everybody says, 'Oh, oh, nerves.' But all we have to do now is birdie the eighteenth hole."

Reading between the lines, you can hear Mauch grasping to hold onto the last strands of hope he had for his team.

Soon enough, almost all those strands were broken.

The Phillies went on to lose all three games in St. Louis.

But, after all this agony, these guys *still* had a chance going into the final two games at Cincinnati. If they could win them both—and the Mets could somehow sweep the Cardinals—they would force a three-team play-off between themselves, the Reds, and St. Louis.

Wouldn't you know it, after a ten-game losing streak, the Phils pulled out a victory in the first tightly contested game against the Reds. Game highlight: A fight almost breaking out when pitcher Chris Short plunked Cardinal Leo Cardenas on the left shoulder. Cardenas called Short a sonofabitch and threatened to hit him with his bat.

He didn't. But he did manage to spark the Phillies out of feeling sorry for themselves. They rallied from behind for a 4-3 victory.

That one weakened strand of hope was still there. Dangling, stretching, wavering...but still holding the entire ballclub—hell, the entire city—of Philadelphia to the playoffs.

When rookie Richie Allen clubbed a double and two homers to lead the Phillies to a 9-0 lead, the knot finally loosened in Gene Mauch's stomach. Their part—the Philadelphia Phillies'—was done. They had blown a huge lead that they shouldn't have. They had pulled out two desperately needed victories to give themselves a chance at survival.

The rest was up to the Mets: They had to beat the Cardinals, for themselves and for the Phils and for the Cincinnati Reds. If they could, maybe there'd be that blue snow just yet.

Alas, this is a tale about losers. That tiny thread of hope Philadelphia clung to is present in the story of every loser. It is a common thin ribbon that weaves its way through each team's history, and it can be seen at the beginning of a fresh season, or at the apex of one played way above the club's talents, or, sometimes, at the end of a glorious one gone awry.

Of course the Cardinals won. That victory provided that last knockout punch for the Phillies, who in the end will be remembered for blowing a six-and-a-half-game lead with twelve to play.

YEAR: 1969
VENUE: Shea Stadium, New York City
EVENT: Chicago Cubs vs. New York Mets pennant race

HERE, IN THE midst of this sports book, we'd like to share a few animal stories.

The first is a long-living, maybe-not-100-percent-factual-but-who-cares legend. On October 6, 1945, the Chicago Cubs were playing in the fourth game of the World Series against the Detroit Tigers. The Cubs had won two of three at Detroit, and were heavily favored to take the Series at home in Wrigley Field's "Friendly Confines." World Series tickets were a hot item; everybody was trying to get their hands on them. One man who did get a pair was William "Billy Goat" Sianis, the owner of a Greek tavern on the North Side. The man got his nickname from the ever-present salt-and-pepper goatee on his face, and from the pet he liked to take with him wherever he went: his goat.

Many times, Sianis had taken his goat to see his beloved Cubs. He usually purchased box seats—one for himself, and one for the goat. But as Sianis walked his goat through the gates of Wrigley before Game 4 of the 1945 World Series, the ushers stopped him.

"No goats," they said.

Sianis couldn't understand it. He was paying for the goat's ticket. He had brought the goat to plenty of games before. What was the problem?

"He smells," the ushers said.

Sianis wished to appeal to Cubs owner P.K. Wrigley.

But Mr. Wrigley only backed his employees, the ushers, up.

"He smells," the ushers reaffirmed.

Well, Sianis was furious. He stood in front of the great classic ballpark, raised both arms, and said, "Cubs, they not gonna win anymore. They never gonna be another World Series played at Wrigley Field."

It's become known as the Billy Goat Curse.

The Tigers won the next three games and took the Series right out from under the Cubbies. Soon after, "Billy Goat" Sianis sent P.K. Wrigley a telegram. It read, "Who smells now?"

Fast forward to 1969—the summer after the Summer of Love. The Beach Boys and Woodstock (weird combo, we know, but you can't argue with history) were setting the mood, Neil Armstrong set foot on the moon, and the Cubs were lighting the National League on fire. This is the setting for the second of our two animal stories. This one's no myth—Ron Santo saw it with his own two eyes.

Santo was the Cubs All-Star third baseman, having a terrific year with a terrific team. The infield was as smooth as any in the league. With Santo and Ernie Banks at the two corners providing the offensive pop, Don Kessinger and Glenn Beckert shored things up down the middle, proving a helluva double-play combination. The outfield featured Billy Williams and Jim Hickman, and behind the plate crouched fan favorite Randy Hundley. (Three of these men—"Mr. Cub" Ernie Banks, Billy Williams and Ron Santo—would have their numbers retired by the Cubs. Guess how many other Cubs have had their numbers retired at Wrigley? None. They were all on the same field in 1969.)

On the mound, things started with the immortal Ferguson Jenkins and his twenty-one wins. But they didn't end there. Bill Hands added twenty more, and Ken Holtzman chipped in with seventeen.

The Cubs started out strong. In their season opener, Ernie Banks hit two homers and the game with the Phillies went into extra innings. In the eleventh inning, trailing, 6-5, pinch-hitter Willie Smith hit a home run with a man aboard to give the Cubs the victory.

Win number one was followed by four straight, and ten of eleven, and from there, the Cubs never looked back.

In retrospect, maybe they should have.

Because the Mets were turning miracles. The New York ballclub had only been around for seven seasons. In '68, they'd finished in ninth place in the National League. Most of their players were young unknowns looking for a star to follow. And they found one in Gil Hodges.

"Gil was the leader of that team and always innings ahead of the game," rightfielder Ron Swoboda said. "The rest of us were too young to lead anybody."

What Hodges understood better than anybody—including Cubs firebrand manager Leo "The Lip" Durocher—was that to get the most out of your players, you have to ease up on them from time to time. So Hodges gave guys days off. He platooned most of his position players. And he used a five-man rotation instead of the accepted four.

Not that he didn't stir the pot once in while. When team batting leader Cleon Jones (.340 for the season) was dogging it one day in July, Hodges slowly, deliberately, walked all the way out to left field and removed Jones from the game for lack of hustle.

The move seemed to push the right buttons with Hodges' young team.

Whaddya know? The once-laughing stock Mets were hanging with the mighty Cubs in the National League East. Sure, they were four games back here, six games back there, five games back over here...in other words, fluctuating daily...but the Amazin' Mets never went away. They never folded. And they rode their powerful—and fresh—young pitchers (led by Tom Seaver, Jerry Koosman, and Tug McGraw, and a fireballer in the bullpen named Nolan Ryan) the whole way.

But few would argue against the fact that the Cubs were simply more talented and more experienced than the Amazin's. And common wisdom had it that they'd pull away in the end.

Sure enough, by August 14, Chicago had a comfortable eight-and-a-half-game lead on the St. Louis Cardinals, while the Mets were 9½ back. There was only a month-and-a-half left to go in the season.

And that's when things started to get interesting.

The Cubs lost a few games, then won six in a row, then went on a four-game losing streak. Meanwhile the Mets got hot. They won five in a row while the Cubs were losing those four. Somehow, when the Cubs came into Shea Stadium in New York City for a two-game series on September 8, their lead over the Mets was only 2½ games.

In the first game, Jerry Koosman beat the Cubs. Tommie Agee, one of those uncelebrated no-name Mets, provided all the offense for the winners with a two-run homer and a double that allowed him to score on a follow-up single. The Cubs lead was 1½.

Now...back to that second animal story.

September 9, 1969. Ron Santo stood in the on-deck circle, waiting his turn to bat at Shea. Suddenly, a cat was loose on the field. A black cat. Uh-oh, bad luck.

The black cat circled Santo. The game stopped, and 56,000 people pointed and cheered the furry little feline. The cat padded around the field for a minute, then headed straight to the front of the Cubs' dugout. There it stopped, at the top of the steps, to look curiously at the collection of Cubbies. It seemed to focus on Leo Durocher. And that's when everyone seemed to know: The Cubs were doomed.

The Billy Goat Curse working through a cat.

Sure enough, the Cubs lost the September 9 game to the Mets, 7-1. The next day, the Mets swept a doubleheader from Montreal. And for the first time since Day One of the 1969 season, the Cubs weren't in first place. They'd held the top spot for 155 straight days.

The rest of the story isn't very dramatic. In fact, it's downright sad. The Cubs ended up losing the division by eight full games. That's a seventeen-and-a-half-game turnaround in six weeks. And that, like the Mets, is truly amazing—even in baseball, where no one's ever seen it all.

The Mets went on to win the World Series. The Cubs went on to be tortured by the legend of William Sianis' Billy Goat Curse.

Three more times—'84, '89, and 2003—they'd be oh-so-close to playing for the baseball championship of the world. And all three times, tragedy would strike, fate would intervene, and the Cubs would not make it to the World Series.

But 1969 was particularly brutal for Chicago Northsiders because it was the last time a Cubs team would sniff the playoffs for the next fifteen years. And that's a long time to stay loyal to a stinky team, right, Mr. Sianis?

21

THE YEAR: 1978
THE VENUE: Fenway Park
THE EVENT: The one-game divisional playoff between the New York Yankees and the Boston Red Sox

BEFORE...THERE was only the passing of seasons. Losing seasons, to be sure, and a lot of them behind the despised Yankees. But there weren't very many Hamlet-level tragedies.

After...there was Buckner and Mookie and Game 6—the ultimate knife-turning/ makes-you-wanna-throw-up moment in all of sports.

But then—right then, in October 1978—there was Bucky Dent, who truly cemented the Curse of the Bambino into sports fans' minds. He plopped it there with a high, lazy fly ball that landed in a net just on the other side of the Green Monster, sending the Yankees on to familiar glory and the Red Sox into their special little cocoon of sorrow and self-loathing.

But Bucky Dent didn't do it all by himself. The guys with the red stockings had plenty of blame on their shoulders.

On July 19, the Sox held a nine-game lead over the best of the rest of the American League. Better yet, they had a fourteen-game lead over those damn Yankees, 1977's World Series Champions.

This was great news to everyone in Boston, considering that since 1920, when the Red Sox traded Babe Ruth to New York, the Yankees had won twenty-one world championships and the Sox had won zero. (We're talking about a hell of a lot of jealousy, envy, and resentment. And, yes, those three words mean the same thing, but in this particular case, there was enough of it to warrant them all.)

Nothing could be sweeter for Bostonians than to look at the league standings in the *Boston Globe* and see the Red Sox at the top, and the Yankees with a double-digit deficit next to their name. With the cushion of a fourteen-game lead, 1978 would be the Red Sox's year. It would be the season where they finally shook off their history of second-place finishes, mixed in with a few tough World Series Game 7 losses, and proudly proved they didn't have to be the Yankees' punching bag.

At least that's the way the fans saw it.

The '78 Sox team was dynamite, top to bottom. DH Carl Yastrzemski, a seasoned, clutch-hitting veteran, was rivaling Ted Williams as the greatest Red Sock of all time. Left fielder Jim Rice proved the perfect hitter for Fenway Park's Green Monster—as powerful a slugger as there was in baseball. Catcher Carlton Fisk was a warrior who never gave up, aching-and-breaking his way to 157 games caught that year. Center fielder Fred Lynn hit the record books as the only player to ever win MVP and Rookie of the Year in the same season (1975). Three years later, he was hitting his stride. Dwight Evans hit twenty-four home runs and played an aggressive right field. Rick Burleson was a scrappy team leader at shortstop, and Butch Hobson provided pop at third base by driving in eighty runs.

On the pitching side, Dennis Eckersley was the ace with twenty wins and sixteen complete games. The rest of the staff included Luis Tiant, in his fifteenth major league season; Mike Torrez, who came over as a free agent from the Yankees after winning two games in the 1977 World Series; and Bill "Spaceman" Lee, an inconsistent, but always-quotable, character.

These Red Sox had sprinted out to a 62-28 record, then faltered a bit in July, mainly due to injuries. Yastrzemski had sprained his wrist and his back. Evans had been beaned in the head. Hobson had a bone chip in his throwing elbow. Burleson battled nagging injuries for three weeks, and without him the Sox were a disappointing 6-12.

At about the same time the Red Sox were having their injury problems, the Yankees were catching fire. Starting on July 19 (the low-point—the fourteen-game deficit), they went on a scorching 35-14 streak. The Yanks surged with confidence, and Reggie Jackson was setting the tone. Streaky as could be, Jackson seemed to streak best when his team's back was against the wall. Mates Thurman Munson and Lou Piniella understood how to let Jackson lead them back from the brink and, by September 7, the Yankees had pulled themselves to within four games of the Red Sox.

But the Red Sox still had command of the American League, especially if you looked a little deeper than the standings. Yes, the lead was a full four games, but more importantly, the two rivals opened a four-game series in Fenway Park that September weekend, where the Sox had a gaudy 52-17 record up to that point in the season.

With the Yankees on their turf, and the season in their control, Sox fans were buzzing with excitement, knowing that by the time the Pinstripes would be catching their plane back to the Bronx, the pennant could be all but wrapped up.

It was the perfect setup for a Boston Massacre.

And that's just what happened. Literally. Because, by the time the Pinstripes *were* catching their plane back to the Bronx, they had outhit the Red Sox in the four-game series, 67 to 30; they had out-batted the Red Sox, .396 to .171; they had outscored the Red Sox, 42 to 9. And they had swept the four-game series—the first Yankees team to do so at Fenway since 1943.

The Yanks had come into Beantown with a four-game deficit. They left with the hearts of BoSox fans. And a tie for the league lead.

Ace Dennis Eckersley summed up the weekend series this way: "When I was a little kid, I wondered how the '64 Phillies could blow the pennant...Now I understand."

And that should have been the end of it.

The Sox should have shriveled up and wilted and melted and died.

They should have given the Yankee steamship a wide berth and watched them sail into the World Series, like so many previous Boston teams had done.

But this team was different. These Red Sox had pride and stubbornness and guts and stick-to-it-iveness—all the qualities needed to crash, and crash hard. These Sox weren't going to let themselves off with that spectacular-but-not-quite-spectacular-enough four-game flameout against the Yanks. They had more anguish in store.

There were still three weeks left in the season.

In the AL office, a coin toss determined where the one-game playoff would take place, if needed, between the Red Sox and the Yankees. The Sox won, and were assured of home-field advantage.

But they lost two of their next three games, and suddenly—finally—the hated Yanks were in first place all alone.

The following weekend, the Red Sox traveled to Yankee Stadium for what appeared to be a crucial three-game series. Any baseball fan knows: In head-to-head matchups like this, a lot of ground can be made up, or a lot of ground can be lost. Sox fans were especially aware of this fact after the previous weekend's massacre.

In the first game, Cy Young-winner Ron Guidry beat Boston's Luis Tiant in a pitcher's duel. In game two, after losing five consecutive down-the-stretch games to the Yankees, the BoSox believed they *needed* a victory—they couldn't afford another "L."

Mike Torrez allowed only one run into the fifth inning, and was clinging to a 2-1 lead with Yankees catcher Thurman Munson at the plate. Reggie Jackson stood in the on-deck circle. That's when Munson ripped a line foul toward him.

In his effort to stop the ball from hitting the fans behind him, Jackson casually and quickly threw up his right hand. Bad move. The ball smashed into his thumb and tore the nail loose. Blood began to show through his batting glove.

The Yanks' trainer taped down the nail, and asked Jackson: "Can you hit?"

"I have no choice," Mr. October replied.

He then walked to the plate and lifted a 2-2 pitch into the right field stands, barely clearing the wall. Mr. October had struck again. Tie game.

The game stayed that way until the bottom of the ninth, when Mickey Rivers led off with a triple. Munson hit a low line drive to left, Jim Rice made a diving catch, and Rivers jogged home for the winning run.

The Yankees led in the standings by 3½.

And *now*, surely, the Red Sox were done.

Nope. Not yet. Because they won the third game in New York, the one that would have put them back 4½ games. Instead, with the win, they were only down 2½.

"Saturday was probably the lowest point in my career," shortstop Rick Burleson said. "But that's what makes this game different. You play every day. You can bounce back."

When the Red Sox won two more, and Guidry and the Yankees lost one, the lead was only 1½. Mike Torrez announced, "This thing ain't over." (That's a bold statement coming from a guy who hadn't won in seven straight starts. He tried to explain his streak as "the damndest thing that ever happened to me, especially at this time of year." But Boston fans had a hard time accepting it.)

With nine games to go, the Sox lost again. Butch Hobson couldn't take it any more: The husky third baseman had committed forty-three errors on the season, and he was making himself sick.

"Take me out," Hobson told his manager, Don Zimmer. "I'm no quitter, but I'm hurting the team, I'm embarrassing the team. I just can't get the ball over to first base. My elbow keeps locking up on me."

It's hard to say if this request was unselfish, cowardly, sad, or humble—or maybe a little bit of each. Whatever you want to call it, Hobson ultimately helped the team. Because the Red Sox didn't lose again.

Dennis Eckersley won two games in that final week of the season, sealing his reputation as the ace of the staff, and ringing up the magical twenty-victory season. He showed a lot of mental courage under fire, too, because he had finalized his divorce just ten days before his penultimate start.

During the clutch eight-game winning streak to close their season, the Red Sox players seemed to be showing everyone that they would be able to overcome the Boston Massacre—that they were different from the Sox teams that had come before.

They also showed signs of irritability, frustration, and toughness. Carl Yastrzemski announced: "I'm tired of people talking about choking.

Nobody is to blame for what happened in the last five weeks. We started the season with twenty-five guys. Twenty-five will stand up if we win. Twenty-five will stand up if we lose." Carlton Fisk tried to explain how important Mike Torrez was to the Sox's chances of winning, but this came out at the end: "I'll be yelling at him. I've tried just about everything. Going out and telling him to reach down sometimes. Talking to him sometimes. Trying to get him mad at the batter, mad at me, mad at anyone. Hate the catcher. Hate me. Throw the ball and hurt me. That's part of it. I'll be yelling. I can't be nice anymore. I'll be yelling."

Going into the last day of the regular season, the Red Sox were still down one game. They had to win, and the Yankees had to lose...and that unlikely scenario—the Yankees were on a six-game tear of a winning streak—would only secure the Sox a chance: a one-game playoff at Fenway to determine the divisional champion.

A prayer to St. Jude, patron saint of lost causes, was posted on the Red Sox clubhouse bulletin board.

Well, the Lost Causes—er, Boston Red Sox—did their part. They were on their way to blanking the Blue Jays, 5-0, at Fenway. It was up to the Cleveland Indians to beat the Yankees and keep the Sox's season alive. And, thankfully, Indians pitcher Rick Waits picked a helluva time to pitch the best game of his life. He tossed a five-hitter, shutting down the vaunted New York offense, and Cleveland won, 9-2.

In Boston, the Fenway Park message board flashed: "SOX NEXT HOME GAME TOMORROW 2:30." And after a pause, it flashed again: "THANK YOU RICK WAITS."

Everything seemed to be falling the Red Sox's way.

Due to the lucky coin toss three weeks earlier, the Sox were set to host the playoff with the Yankees at Fenway Park, where they had won six in a row and had gone 33-3 down the stretch. New York broadcaster Phil Rizzuto said: "I just can't get myself ready for this, going up to Boston." Maybe the Yankees felt the same way. Maybe this was the year Boston would turn their second-place fortunes around. Maybe St. Jude *was* working for the Sox.

The night before the playoff, tensions were running high, even for the usually confident world champion Yankees. Goose Gossage, their intimidating relief pitcher, couldn't sleep. He kept imagining himself facing Yaz with two outs in the ninth. Lou Piniella couldn't sleep either. After a few hours mulling things over in his hotel room, he dressed and took a walk over to Daisy Buchanan's, a nearby bar.

Piniella ordered a Jack Daniel's and water, and started to feel guilty about leaving the peace and quiet of his hotel room the night before the most exciting game of his career. He looked around the bar. To his surprise, Thurman Munson, Graig Nettles and several other teammates were looking right back at him.

"We can't sleep, either," Nettles told Piniella.

By the time dawn arrived on the day of the season-deciding game, police on horseback were already gathered outside the stadium to control the beer-drinking crowd. Inside Fenway, the teams were gearing up: taking batting practice, fielding grounders, putting on uniforms, checking gear. Yankee Mickey Rivers noticed a chip in the bat he and Bucky Dent normally used. Rivers told Dent, "Don't use that chipped bat anymore. I've got a new one that feels good."

"No," Dent said. "I'll stick with the old one."

The shortstop probably figured it wouldn't make much of a difference. He batted ninth in the Yankees lineup, carried an average of .243 into the tiebreaker, and had hit only four homers and thirty-seven RBIs all year. And by the time he popped up to Jim Rice in the third inning, the Red Sox led, 1-0, on a Yastrzemski home run to right field. In the sixth inning, Boston added another run on a double by Rick Burleson, a Jerry Remy sacrifice, and an RBI single by Rice.

The Yankees had only managed two hits against Torrez (perhaps Fisk's yelling was helping?) and trailed 2-0 going into the seventh.

Torrez got Graig Nettles out. But the next two hitters ripped singles and stood as the tying runs out on the bases. Brian Doyle, the second baseman, was next up. Yankee manager Bob Lemon elected to pinch-hit for him with powerful first baseman/DH Jim Spencer. But Spencer flied out, and the decision to lift Doyle meant that light-hitting Bucky Dent would have to remain in the game for the duration. He would be the next batter up in that seventh inning, with two on and two out, down 2-0.

Didn't look good for the Yankees.

Looked pretty darn good for the Red Sox.

Dent took the first pitch for a ball. He swung at the second pitch, which he fouled straight down and slammed off his left ankle. This was unfortunate, because Dent usually wore a shin guard to protect the area where he had incurred preseason surgery. That playoff day, however, he wasn't wearing the guard. And when the ball hit him, he began hopping around in pain. The team trainer came out to the batter's box to spray painkiller (ethyl chloride) on the sore spot. In the dugout, manager Bob Lemon wished he had another pinch-hitter for Dent right now. And in the on-deck circle, Mickey Rivers decided to take advantage of the pause in action.

He turned to the batboy: "Get that other bat."

He turned to Dent: "Hey, homey, you're using the wrong bat. Use this one."

Dent took the new lumber from the batboy and stepped back into the box. Throughout the delay, Torrez had tossed the ball easily back and forth with shortstop Burleson. Now, he had to refocus back on home plate, back on the task at hand, back on light-hitting Bucky Dent.

On the first pitch after the delay, Torrez tried to throw a fastball inside. But it wasn't fast enough; nor was it inside enough.

Dent swung, and sent a rising fly ball toward the Green Monster in left field. The ball kept rising, and as Dent rounded first base, the crowd went sickeningly silent. He looked up the baseline to second-base umpire Al Clark, and realized Clark was waving his right arm in a circle. Home run.

None of the 32,925 fans packed into Fenway could move; hell, they could hardly breathe. Like they just got kicked in the stomach.

The rest of the game has been mostly forgotten. (As it turned out, the Yankees scored two more runs to build a 5-2 lead. Then, the Red

Sox responded with two runs of their own. Then, Goose Gossage's imagination became a reality: He faced Yaz with the tying runner on third in the ninth, but he got the Red Sox great to pop up to Nettles at third to end the game.) Forgotten, except by Red Sox fans who relive it in their nightmares.

But the image of Bucky Dent hustling around first base, hoping for a double off the wall, realizing the ball had landed in the net, sucking all hope out of Fenway Park...that lives on and on. It has become the moment that forced Boston fans to admit to themselves that they might very well be cursed; the moment that cemented the Curse of the Bambino into every sports fan's consciousness.

Time and habitual second-place finishes may have come before, and Bill Buckner may have come after. But Bucky Dent...he was pure anguish.

22

THE YEAR: 1996
THE VENUE: Augusta National golf course, Augusta Georgia
THE EVENT: The Masters

IF GREG NORMAN were looking for bad omens, he might have noted that on April 14, 1912, the *Titanic,* an unsinkable ship, sank like the million-ton brick it was. Eighty-four years later, Norman would have a very similar feeling.

For being the number-one golfer in the world, Norman had suffered his share of brutal defeats—defeats that came after he had cruised along on top of leader boards. He sort of had a reputation for it.

Particularly at Augusta.

In '81, he blew a big lead on the final day and watched Tom Watson put on the green jacket.

In '86, he became a spectator as forty-six-year-old Jack Nicklaus stole his lead and his spotlight.

In '87, local-boy Larry Mize chipped in from hell-and-gone to snatch victory in a playoff.

And in 1995, Ben Crenshaw out-putted him all Sunday to ensure Norman remained always-a-bridesmaid-never-the-bride.

All told, seven times Norman carried the lead from Saturday into Sunday at one of golf's four majors; he'd only won one of them.

But on the April 14 in question, there was unlikely to be any thoughts of the *Titanic.* That Sunday at the Masters, all of Greg Norman's previous crash-and-burns looked to be buried beneath the glorious runaway victory he had set himself up for.

Just the previous night, Norman relaxed in the non-champions locker room. (Augusta National segregated everything—including its winners and its losers.) He had reason to be relaxed—it's called a six-stroke lead. And as he slouched in a chair, a friend pointed out: "Your last night in *this* locker room."

Norman laughed—a genuine, hearty laugh. No nervousness. "Damn, I hope so," he said.

Then, this, from a well-meaning British friend, who grabbed Norman by both shoulders and shook him: "Greg, old boy, there's no way you can [bleep] this up now!"

And the Brit was right. On that third day, Norman had already held off a charging Nick Faldo. In fact, he not only held him off, he increased his lead from four to six strokes heading into the final round. Even Faldo expected to lose. So sure was he that Norman would be victorious that he lackadaisically arrived at the course a half-hour behind schedule, a move that reeked of "Why bother?"

Everybody seemed to be pulling for Norman, fellow players and Augusta natives alike. "I'd like to see ol' Norman win," one local said. "He's just had this thing slud out from under him one too many times."

Even the golfing gods seemed to be on his side. Example: On Wednesday, Norman's back hurt so badly that he left his practice session two hours early; barely able to take a half-swing. But Freddie Couples—'92 Masters winner—called up out of the blue and offered to send over his back therapist. By tee time Thursday, Norman was feeling good enough to start his course-record-tying round, sixty-three.

Another example: On Friday, at the always-tricky par-three twelfth, Norman hit a shot that, in a fair world, would have been wet; he struck it poorly, it caught a strong gust, drifted in flight, hit a hard bank, and rolled toward the famous Rae's Creek.

But it stopped, only inches from the water hazard.

Gods a-smiling. Norman's time in the sun.

But on Sunday, he took his first swing. And hooked it. Hooked it bad. The drive sailed into the trees, leading to a bogey on the first hole.

It got worse. On number three, Norman got a lucky par, making it just about as difficult for himself as he possibly could. He took another bogey on number four, and on eight, he hit a horrendous—barely watchable—hook.

Meantime, Faldo was plugging along. Par after par after par—reliable as Old. He birdied the sixth and the eighth with strong putts. Result: Norman's lead stood at three strokes.

And that was when you could hear it, ever so faintly, if you really listened: "Iceberg. Dead ahead."

Norman hit his wedge to within six feet of the pin on the ninth green. But the damn ball slid...and slid...and slid...*thirty yards* back toward him. Norman couldn't save par from there. He pulled out a pretty impressive bogey, considering the awful, gut-wrenching backward roll. But his lead was now only two.

The tenth offered him one of the more simple uphill chips anyone is likely to see at Augusta. It's where Norman crashed and burned. It's where he sent his chip shot eight feet past the whole and, of course, missed the par putt coming back.

One stroke lead.

Nick Price, Norman's closest friend on the tour, who had been watching in the clubhouse until that point, got up from his chair. Pale. "I can't stand to watch," he said, and headed for his car.

Understandable, Nick. But it was one of those things: You know you shouldn't be gaping, but you can't stop. Sort of like going to the same disaster movie over and over again ...

Hole eleven. Tee shot—perfect. Approach shot—perfect. Ten-foot putt— lips out. Okay. Easy three-footer for par, right? Uh-uh. Missed it.

And what once was a six-stroke lead had turned into a tie.

With seven brutal holes still to go. Starting with Number twelve.

Remember that stroke of luck Norman had on Friday, when his poorly misplayed shot stopped just short of the water's edge of Rae's Creek? That was twelve. This par-three hole is an absolute witch as is, but if you don't get the help of the gods, you're in *serious* trouble.

Greg Norman was in trouble. Tight. Out of his normal routine. Analyzing every shot way too long. Playing not to lose. Headed for disaster.

At the edge of the gallery behind him, Norman's thirteen-year-old daughter tried to calm her mommy down. Both were praying. "It's gonna be *all right*, Mom," said daughter.

Wishful thinking.

Her daddy pushed his shot past Faldo's ball—as it sat safely on the green—and the whole family watched as it rolled right off into the pond. Penalty shots were assessed. Double-bogey recorded. Norman's fifth straight five on the scorecard.

For the first time all week, Norman didn't lead this Masters tournament. Now Faldo, unbelievably, held *a two-shot* lead. In five holes, Norman gave him six strokes.

Norman and Faldo traded birdies and pars and birdies, respectively, at thirteen, fourteen, and fifteen. On that last one, Norman missed an eagle by a smidgen with a chip from just off the green. As the ball missed the hole, he fell back on his haunches and looked up to the sky, then let himself be toppled backwards by the oh-so-closeness of the moment.

In that instant, he seemed to realize that the end was near.

No, he seemed to realize that the end probably really happened when he chipped past the hole. "I needed to hit a hook in there," Norman would say later of his first shot on Number sixteen. "I sure hooked it."

Yep. Hooked it right into the water. Another double-bogey. Faldo led by four.

And now he—Faldo—in a cruel twist, cruised his way through the final three holes and into the clubhouse. He—Faldo—ended up with that fashion no-no of a green jacket, with the prime seat at the champion's dinner.

"I screwed up," Norman, who finished five strokes behind Faldo, said at his press conference, smiling. "But losing this Masters is not the end of the world. I let this one get away, but I still have a pretty good life. I'll wake up tomorrow, still breathing."

That's more than you can say for a lot of the other people who've taken rides on sinking ships.

23

THE YEAR: 1993
THE VENUE: Louisiana Superdome
THE EVENT: The NCAA Basketball Championship Game, North Carolina Tar Heels vs. Michigan Wolverines

IN OCTOBER, just before the start of the 1992-'93 college basketball season, Chris Webber told a story to a reporter on media day. He described a scene when, as a twelve-year-old, he showed up for his first day of AAU practice with a team of Detroit-area kids. He hadn't played much basketball up till then, and he arrived wearing a Hawaiian shirt and shorts. At basketball practice. Inside a hot gym.

All the other players teased him mercilessly. One of them—a skinny kid named Jalen Rose—even went so far as to tell Webber, "You've got the sorriest game I've ever seen."

It was the first time on a basketball court, Webber recalled, that he felt like everyone was laughing at him.

It wouldn't be the last.

Flash forward to March 1993. A whole season had gone by, and Chris Webber's Michigan Wolverines were one of the last two teams standing. Came down to a national championship game between them and the North Carolina Tar Heels.

For Michigan, the previous two seasons had been one wild ride, mostly due to the phenomenon that was the Fab Five. After Michigan's sub-par 14-15 season in 1991, the Fab Five—a brash, precocious, oh-so-talented group of blue-chip freshmen, considered by many to be the "greatest recruiting class of all time"—arrived on campus.

Webber was the centerpiece of the group—a smooth, effortless player, full of style and charisma. He brought Michael Jordan's shaved head to the college game; he wore baggy shorts and black socks, which no one else did at the time; he grinned more than he should have, and gave the impression that he was having way too much fun while he ripped your heart out with his killer game.

But he wasn't the only Michigan force to be reckoned with. There was Juwan Howard—a quiet, physical post player who could destroy opponents with his fundamentals. There were Jimmy King and Ray Jackson—incredibly athletic wing players with an open-court game that begged, "How would you prefer me to dunk on you *this time?*" And there was aforementioned wise-guy Jalen Rose—an untraditional bean pole of a point guard; 6-feet-9-inches, left-handed, with crazy ball control and fantastic court vision.

From the time they set foot in Ann Arbor, the Fab Five were starters. In 1992, they did what no other team of all-freshmen starters had done before: They made it to the NCAA Championship Game. Sure, they had lost to Duke, but how could anyone have expected them to beat such an experienced, tournament-tested team, with the likes of Christian Laettner, Bobby Hurley, Grant Hill, et al?

No, playing in that championship only increased the sensation of Webber and his mates. The game was the highest-rated college basketball broadcast ever, with 21 million homes tuned in. It even led kids everywhere to start wearing extra-baggy shorts. Suddenly, Bic-ed heads became the new afro. And Webber, Rose and Howard jerseys and shorts flew off retail store shelves all over the country. In fact, Michigan's athletic royalties more than tripled in the two years the Fab Five were around—from $2 million in pre-Fab 1990-91 to $6.2 million in '93.

In their sophomore season, expectations were higher yet. And the Fab Five met them. They were fun to watch, mostly because they weren't businesslike. These weren't professionals on the court. They were nineteen- and twenty-year-old kids, slapping fives, dancing, chest-bumping and trash-talking. They played with an infectious joy. They played to showcase. They played to win.

By the time that championship game versus North Carolina rolled around, the super-sophs had proved that their freshman success was no fluke. With a 31-4 record, they had placed second in the Big Ten (behind an Indiana team featuring Big Ten Player of the Year Calbert Cheaney), and were coming off a composed, impressive overtime win against Number One seed Kentucky in the national semis.

But Dean Smith's North Carolina team was no slouch. It, too, had earned a top seed in March's Madness. It, too, had secured a spectacular recruiting class comprised of five Top 100 players, including Eric Montross, Derrick Phelps, Brian Reese and Pat Sullivan.

But most importantly, North Carolina had Dean Smith—the winningest coach in NCAA Division I history.

Smith had taken a Tar Heels team to the Final Four in four consecutive decades. This included his 1982 championship team, with a hotshot freshman named Michael Jordan. That year's Final Four had also been played at the Superdome in New Orleans, and it was decided on a critical fluke mistake: Georgetown's Fred Brown, in his haste to get rid of the ball as the clock dwindled, passed directly to North Carolina's James Worthy, who was standing on the wing all by himself. The inexplicable pass assured that Jordan's jumper with sixteen seconds left would be the game-clincher; it handed Smith his first long-awaited championship; and some say it was proof that the spirits who haunt the city of New Orleans play favorites.

Ten years later, Michigan-versus-North Carolina was shaping up to be another classic, but in its own unique way. This was not a punch-for-punch battle between two evenly matched heavyweights. Instead, it was a herky-jerky, lurching game of runs, with drastic swings alternately favoring both sides. The Tar Heels went up by five. Michigan countered, and suddenly led by ten. North Carolina came out of the corner, swinging, to go back up by eight.

But with 4:31 left, Michigan took a four-point lead, which would be its largest lead for the remainder of the game. Suddenly, Final Four MVP Donald Williams—armed with one of the most automatic sweet shots in the history of basketball—swished his fifth three-pointer of the game (on seven attempts). George Lynch—the only senior on the court—blocked a Michigan shot. And Derrick Phelps hit a running layup to give North Carolina a one-point lead. A turnaround hit by Lynch put the Heels up by three. When Jalen Rose got careless with the ball in traffic, Donald Williams intercepted his pass and hit Montross on a breakaway for a monstrous slam.

Michigan needed something, and they got it: a mid-range jumper by Ray Jackson.

That's when they called a timeout, trailing 72-69.

This was their last timeout, and the Michigan coaches told them so in the huddle. It would have been nice to have one more, with forty-six seconds still remaining in the game, but the Wolverines had wasted a timeout early in the second half when Juwan Howard couldn't get the ball in to Jalen Rose within the allotted five seconds. Burned play; burned timeout.

No more left in case of an end-of-the-game emergency.

Coming out of the huddle, North Carolina ran a sloppy inbounds play, which the Wolverines defensed perfectly. Reese stepped over the out-of-bounds line as he tried to receive the ball, and in doing so gave the possession back to Michigan before any time ran off the clock. Rose rushed a three-pointer to try to tie the score, and missed badly. But old reliable Webber was there to gather in the rebound and put it back in for two.

The Tar Heels lead was down to one—with only twenty seconds to play.

Michigan fouled Pat Sullivan to stop the clock.

Sullivan made the first foul shot. He missed the second. And Webber pulled down his game-high eleventh rebound.

But here's where the ghosts of New Orleans may have started to play their favorites again.

As the rest of the players retreated downcourt, Webber—alone and in front of God and 20.7 million viewers—pivoted and dragged his foot for what seemed like a country mile. *Then* he began dribbling.

Every single person on the Tar Heel bench leapt up and cried, "Traveling!"

But no whistle blew.

Webber brought the ball up the court, with his Wolverines down by two, and a 50/50 chance to tie or win the National Championship.

15...14...13...12...11...

Webber stopped dribbling, hounded by Phelps and Lynch in a classic double-team—all arms and jumping legs and grabbing and shouting. "Ball! Ball! Ball! Ball!"

So Webber did what he had been drilled to do when the possession is critical, the game's winding down, and defenders are scratching and clawing at you to steal the ball away.

He called timeout.

Only...Michigan didn't have any more timeouts to call.

Deep in the college basketball rulebook, there's a punishment for such an unlikely crime—an automatic technical foul with two free throws and possession of the ball awarded to the other team.

To see Chris Webber's body language in the split-second after he realized his own mistake was to watch a twenty-year-old kid get crushed, as if by a gigantic hammer of embarrassment and anger and I-don't-know-whether-to-defend-myself-or-run-away-or-argue-or-cry-to-mama. He might as well have been wearing a Hawaiian shirt and shorts right there, in the middle of his trend-setting Fab Five teammates with their shiny yellow uniforms and North Carolina's slick powder-blue-with-plaid-trim garb.

Sadder still, Webber had to stay out on the court, with those awful slouched shoulders and that pitiful blank look on his face that said, "Please get me out of here." Until the game finally concluded—11 seconds and four free throws later.

It was only afterward, when most people had cleared out of the Superdome and he walked down a lonely corridor with his bag slung over his shoulder and a baseball cap pulled low on his head, that Chris Webber's honest emotion came rushing out. After a few remaining fans yelled, "That's all right, Chris!" and "Hang in there, Chris," Webber found himself in the assuring arms of his father, Mayce, and one of his brothers.

That's where his bag dropped to the floor, his shoulders slouched even more, his head hung a little lower, and he started sobbing uncontrollably.

Some say Webber got what he deserved after having just traveled so blatantly without penalty.

Some say he should have been listening more closely during the time-out at forty-six seconds left, when his coaches warned that there were no more to be called.

Others blame it all on the ghosts of New Orleans, and say it was out of Chris Webber's hands.

Playing the blame game can be a tough proposition, but this much can be said of losers: Sometimes, your opponent is more talented than you and takes advantage of your weakness. Sometimes, you have an off day, and the game takes advantage of you. And sometimes, those pesky things known as "the rules of the game" can sneak up and bite you.

Chris Webber got bit.

24

THE YEAR: 1999
THE COURSE: Scotland's historic, revered, stubborn Carnoustie
THE EVENT: the 128th British Open, golf's oldest championship

FOR SEVENTY-ONE of the tournament's seventy-two holes, Jean Van de Velde charmed the crowd and the course. A relative unknown (his best finish prior to that '99 British Open was a tie for fifth at The Qatar Masters), he captured the crowd's—and his competitors'—attention by playing the role of flamboyant Frenchman, full of cavalier style and relaxed humor. Van de Velde's golf game was the same—uncautious, unflappable, attacking. In other words: Who ever heard of laying up?

And he led. His name had been on top of the leader board for most of the four-day tournament. A remarkable story, really. He wasn't Woods, Mickelson, or Duval. He wasn't familiar, like Monty or Vijay or Nick Price. But his name was about to be etched onto golf's version of The Stanley Cup—the Old Claret Jug.

Wasn't it? Surely, a three-stroke lead *on the very last hole of the tournament* is safe. Surely, any decent high-school golfer could play this last hole in six strokes or better. Surely, even Bill Murray—in full *Caddyshack* greenskeeper mode, using only that rake from the "Dalai Lama himself" scene—could hole out the par-four in double bogey. Because that's all Van de Velde needed. A six. A big, fat, hideous double bogey. And we'd be calling him one of life's winners.

To be fair, the last hole at Carnoustie is a 480-yarder with a wee burn that crosses the fairway a few times. If you hit a slice or a fade, chances are decent you'll end up in a ridiculous bunker that you actually have to crawl in and out of.

But Van de Velde was a pro. And his first major victory was his. All he had to do was hit a four-iron that landed safely in front of that first burn crossing. From there, he could hit another easy four-iron that would land *safely*—that's the key word here—in front of the third crossing of the burn; then a nice little wedge shot to the green—anywhere on the green; and, from there, three-putt his way to everlasting glory. (Not to mention the ten-year PGA Tour exemption, which means that he could play in any tour event he wanted—without having to qualify—for a decade. Translation: Guaranteed money to play golf.)

So what was that thing he pulled out of his bag? The big head didn't look like the four- or five-iron the hole demanded. No, irons are shinier. They're not so wide. That looked more like...like...a driver. A driver? Caddy, where were you? To take that driver out of his hands. To hide it. To throw it in the nearest lake. Whatever. But your job was to *not* let Van de Velde use it. He was bringing the ire of the golf gods down upon himself. He was asking for trouble.

Of course, he got it. The trouble. Just like he asked for. He pushed his tee shot way, way right, almost to the tee box on seventeen. Now he faced 240 yards of swaying Carnoustie heather and wee crossing burn to get to the pin. But he hadn't really lost a shot yet. He didn't go into the burn, have to take a drop, and risk strokes. He could still pitch out onto the fairway, still hit wedge onto the dance floor, and *still*, amazingly, three-putt for the win. And everlasting glory.

The thing is, it's really hard to hit a nice easy wedge with a *two-iron*. That's the club Van de Velde pulled out of his bag. That's the club he used—not to pitch out onto the fairway—to go for the green.

This is where most people started to get that uncomfortable knot in their stomachs. You know the one? You got it when Mikey kept calling Nikki's answering machine in *Swingers*. You just knew he was going to keep shoveling and shoveling until he was completely buried. You almost had to cover your eyes. Same with Van de Velde and his two-iron.

Of course, it sailed way, way, *way* right. So far right it hit the grandstand, bounced over the burn, and ended up in heather high enough to hide Winona Ryder. The next hack was exactly that—a hack. He might as well have pulled out a machete. The ball went directly *into* the burn.

Now Van de Velde was laying three. He'd already eliminated the part where he three-putted his way to everlasting glory. What's worse, his ball was mostly covered by water. The six-foot-high creek wall was directly in front of it. And this Frenchman who was once flamboyant, cavalier, and attacking had become a pathetic, desperate, car wreck that we couldn't take our eyes off of. Look: He took off his shoes and socks, he rolled up his pantlegs. He actually was going to try to hit his fourth shot out of the water.

You couldn't help it: *Please don't do it. Have some pride, man.*

Oh, thank God. He changed his mind. He put his socks back on. He took a drop back into the haggis, then easily hit it over the burn. And straight into a sand trap. That was his fifth shot. Still not on the green. Van de Velde—remember when he was looking at a three-putt?—now had to get up and down out of a greenside bunker just to make a playoff with Justin Leonard and some never-before-heard-of guy named Paul Lawrie.

Somehow, he did it, making a ridiculously ballsy seven-foot putt. But, it was obvious that his nerves were shot. He was frazzled. Not flamboyant, cavalier, or even remotely confident. And golf, perhaps more than any other game, requires, demands—no, *needs*—confidence.

Van de Velde ended up losing the playoff to the Scotsman Lawrie. It's too sad to recount the details. Nonetheless, Jean Van de Velde secured his place in history not as a second-place finisher, but as "that guy who blew the British Open."

FREAK SHOWINGS

25

THE YEAR: 1982
THE VENUE: Schaefer Stadium in Foxboro, Massachusetts
THE EVENT: An AFC East regular-season matchup between the Miami Dolphins and the New England Patriots

A NOR'EASTER, a Zamboni, a criminal and a timeout. Those were the ingredients that combined to cook the Miami Dolphins on December 12, 1982.

"Cook" might be the wrong word, considering the game we're talking about took place in New England's Schaefer Stadium in the dead of winter; there was no heat involved—only cold-weather element.

The day before the big AFC East rivalry game, it had rained from morning to night, covering the Astroturf with water. But that was only the beginning. Because Saturday, the temperature dropped overnight and the swamped turf was suddenly an ice rink—one solid, slippery sheet.

Then the Nor'easter came.

Sunday morning, while New Englanders were trying to get back and forth to church, the snows accumulated...and accumulated...and piled up...and up...and up. Nor'easter? Hell, this was more like the North Pole.

The NFL didn't care. The game was still on.

Predictably, both teams had a hard time running. And when we say "running," we don't mean "gaining rushing yards against the other team's defense." We mean, literally, *running*. Quarterbacks slid backwards after the snap. Running backs went down face-first. Lineman pushed off and lost their feet underneath them. And receivers, well, the minute they tried to button-hook...splat.

Kickers had the worst time of it. Both the Dolphins' and the Pats' place-kicker missed an attempt. The Patriots' John Smith explained his: "The first kick I tried…[Coach] Meyer hadn't decided whether to run the ball with [fullback] Mosi [Tatupu] or try a field goal. Matt Cavanaugh [the holder] and I couldn't even find a place to kick from. If you cleared away the snow, you couldn't stand on the ice. When I tried to kick, I slipped, the ball hit John Hannah in the back, and we didn't score."

FYI: John Hannah was an offensive lineman on Smith's own team.

For the most part, the game was played like that: Errors everywhere. Slipups all over the place. Gaffes too many to count.

Neither squad made it anywhere near an end zone. The Patriots would have the ball, slosh around for a while, end up losing yards, and then punt it over to the Dolphins. Then the Fish would go on offense, slide, fumble and stumble themselves backward, then turn it back over to the Pats.

Somehow in the midst of all this, Patriots fullback Tatupu racked up 81 yards rushing on thirteen carries. (It would earn him the nickname "The Snowin' Samoan.") Fellow running back Mark Van Eeghen gained 100 yards on twenty-two attempts. These guys weren't going backwards; they just weren't going far enough forward to change the scoreboard zeros.

Fans in the stands had a hard time deciphering exactly where, on the field, the ball was being marked after each play. The yard lines, you see, were obscured by all that white fluff nature had piled down on them. And although the fans had it rough, the refs had it worse. Short-yardage situations were an absolute witch, accuracy-wise, in Foxboro that day. The only reprieve came in the form of a Zamboni-like snow plow: During each and every timeout, twenty-four-year-old Mark Henderson would drive his John Deere-with-attached-snow-plow out to the relevant play zone to clear the yard lines, mostly for the sake of the refs' sanity.

The game was surely headed for a scoreless tie at the end of regulation. Then, overtime.

But with 4:45 left on the clock, New England found itself on the Miami 16-yard line. The Patriots' drive had stalled there, but they were within field-goal range. So Coach Ron Meyer called timeout in order to give John

Smith, already 0-for-1 on the day, a chance to properly clear a patch of turf on the snow-covered field.

"The first kick I tried, I only had about ten seconds to prepare," said Smith. That's the one that ended up in John Hannah's back.

This time, with the game on the line, Meyer was going to make sure his kicker had plenty of time to find firm footing. At least, as firm as could be scouted and cleared during an NFL timeout.

"I saw John Smith on his hands and knees trying to get the snow cleared, and all of a sudden it hit me," explained Meyer years later. "Why not send a snow plow out there?"

So instead of going through strategy or offering his kicking team a pep talk, Meyer spent the timeout walking up and down the sideline, looking for the operator of the John Deere. When he finally found him, Meyer told Henderson to clear off a spot on the field for Smith to kick from.

Here's what Meyer didn't know about the John Deere operator: He happened to be serving a fifteen-year sentence for burglary at Norfolk State Prison, and was working on the Schaefer Stadium maintenance crew as part of a work-release program.

This means two things: One, Henderson was really good at following orders. (And, make no mistake, he jumped right on Meyer's order—no hesitation.) Two, he had a sneaky streak in him, like any good lawbreaker needs. So when he drove his snow plow out onto the field, he made it look like he was just doing his job—clearing the yard lines every five yards, ho-hum. Then—just as he was passing the spot where Smith and his holder Cavanaugh had been digging through the ice to create a spot for Smith's non-kicking foot—Henderson veered off his straight path and gave a clean sweep to the area.

Henderson left behind a perfect swath of green SuperTurf between the 23- and 25-yard lines.

That was easy.

Pretty tricky, too.

And if you look up the transitive verb "to trick" in the dictionary, you'll find a synonym: Cheat.

Cheating, Captain Obvious would like to point out, is pretty much universally frowned upon in the sporting world.

But the Dolphins could only watch helplessly as Jailbird Henderson and his John Deere executed the best sweep Foxboro fans had seen in years. Miami defensive tackle Bob Baumhower said it best: "I saw him coming, but what was I supposed to do? No way I'm going to take on a plow."

Right.

So play resumed. The officials weren't sure what to do, since there was no in-game illegality to what Henderson had done. Smith lined up on the green turf, took his normal approach to the kick, planted his foot *firmly*, and booted the game-winning 33-yarder.

Dolphins coach Don Shula was incensed. In his post-game press conference, he said, "Somebody in New England is going to have to live with it. Whoever ordered it or told the guy to do it has got to think long and hard about the ramifications of something like that."

And he's right.

But sometimes in sports, the home team gets the advantage. And sometimes—especially in *pro* sports—what separates the winner from the loser is not talent as much as it is that little stretch of time, brief as it might be, when everything—in this case, the storm, the tractor, the jailbird, and the stopped clock—comes together for one side and works together to bury the other.

26

THE 1985 ST. LOUIS Cardinals were a hard team to put a finger on. Were they eccentric-ly great? Or were they arrogant wackos?

"The Nuthouse Gang," people called them. (A call-back to the 1930s Cardinals—the Gas House Gang—led by Dizzy Dean and Ducky Medwick and Ripper Collins.) And the '85 Cards' nickname couldn't have been more appropriate. Quite simply, the engaging cast of characters—at times out-rageous, moody, humble, fun-loving, competitive, and cocky—was, from many an observer's perspective...well, nuts.

The team's shortstop, known as "The Wizard," did backflips on his way out to his position (Ozzie Smith). Its hit-machine left fielder had silly-looking bowed legs that looked even sillier in tight baseball pants and stirrups (Willie McGee). Its quiet rookie leadoff man stole bases in big bunches—like they were extra mints at the exit of an Italian restaurant (Vince Coleman). Its second baseman (Tommy Herr) played like a middle linebacker. And its ace pitcher (John Tudor) snapped reporters' heads off, i.e., "What do you need to get a media credential, a driver's license?"

Need more characters? How about a Dominican pitcher with fire in both his fastball and his temperament (Joaquin Andujar); a first baseman who intimidated with his size and his cool/confident attitude (Jack Clark, who once said, "I have two goals. The first is to play in the World Series and the second is to hit .400. And I think I'll do both someday."); and, at the top of the food chain, a manager who rarely gave credit to the teams that beat his, and who made plenty of excuses when his own guys lost (Whitey Herzog). Whitey was so disliked by certain media members that he was called a "rodent-at-arms" by no less a publication than *Sports Illustrated*.

As eccentric as The Nuthouse Gang was, though, they could flat-out *play*. With a regular season record of 101-61—the best in the bigs—nobody could argue that. Willie McGee led the NL in hits (216), batting average (.353) and triples (18). Vince Coleman led the majors in stolen bases with an outlandish 110. John Tudor led the league in shutouts (10). Five Cardinals played on the All-Star team (Smith, Herr, Clark, Andujar, McGee). The Wizard of Oz and Willie McGee were Gold Glovers; Coleman won Rookie of the Year honors; Herzog was Manager of the Year; and McGee garnered MVP.

As the Cards rolled into the playoffs, they rode a 24-12 hot streak during the final two months of the season. They promptly—surprisingly—lost the first two games of the National League Championship Series to the Los Angeles Dodgers, but then, just as promptly, won four straight to gallop into the World Series.

Their opponent-to-be was the Kansas City Royals, the Cardinals' instate rival. The Royals were a scrappy bunch, led by hard-nosed third baseman George Brett and composed twenty-one-year-old Cy Young-winner Bret Saberhagen. The "other Missouri team" had gutted out a win in the ALCS, coming back from a 3-1 series deficit to knock out the Toronto Blue Jays. In stark opposition to the Cardinals swagger, the Royals limped onto the biggest stage in all of baseball.

The seven-game set would not leave the Missouri boundaries, so the media dubbed it the "Show-Me Series." And from the beginning, the whole thing looked like a rockin' Redbird good time.

That's because the only relief the Royals had—after they had put forth so much effort to get past the Blue Jays—was the fact that they'd be playing the first two games in their home ballpark, Royals Stadium.

Unfortunately for the Royals, they gave up that relief by blowing both games: 3-1 and 4-2, respectively.

When the two teams traveled back to St. Louis for Games 3, 4, and 5, a bright red celebration greeted them. The Cards and their fans knew that they needed to win only two of the three home games—their average for the season—to pop the champagne that goes along with being world champions. A downtown, noontime rally the day of the first St. Louis home game seemed more like a coronation than anything, with banners that read "TURN OUT THE LIGHTS, THE FAT LADY IS SINGING" and the like. By the time team owner Gussie Busch—who made his fortune as Budweiser Braumeister—trotted out onto the field behind his world-famous team of Clydesdales, the most appropriate song to fit the mood would have been Budweiser's theme, "Here Comes the King." Oh, wait—that's exactly what was played. But was it for Busch or his Cardinals? Or both?

The Nuthouse Gang lost Game 3, won Game 4, and was just one game from the red-ribbon world championship.

St. Louis—perhaps the best baseball town in America, with its long history of Cardinal success and its appreciative, knowledgeable fans—was ready to bask in its team's glory.

But KC's Saberhagen—and it was hard to tell if he was being facetious or cavalier when he said this—warned: "They've fallen right into our trap. We've got them right where we want them."

Now, in every professional sport—whether it be the World Series, the Stanley Cup playoffs, the Super Bowl, or the NBA Finals—whenever there's a chance for one team to clinch a championship, preparations must be made in the celebrators' locker room. Because champagne will be spilled. Cigars will be smoked and ashed. Inanimate objects will be thrown. So...prior to that possible clinching game, a crew of stadium workers will cover the lockers with plastic sheets and will erect a victory stand where players, coaches, general managers and owners will pass the trophy along to one another and thank God and their wives and their kids for helping them along the path to victory.

This is what was happening in the Cardinals locker room before Game 5. And the Royals knew it.

On the field, the Royals won easily, 6-1. Danny Jackson—their number-three pitcher—held the Cardinals' high-powered offense to five hits. Willie Wilson ripped a two-run triple in the second inning that turned out to be all the offense KC would need—even though it got plenty more.

The plastic draping and the victory stand had to be torn down; the Series was heading back on I-70 to Kansas City, where the stuff was reconstructed in the visitors' locker room in Royals Stadium before Game 6—another chance for the Cardinals to clinch, another chance to spray the bubbly.

Alas, that Game 6 would turn out to be one of the most memorable in the Fall Classic's history, combining excellent play, suspense, courage, and more than a little luck. Plus, one of the most controversial endings. Ever.

It was a sphincter-tightening pitcher's duel for the first eight innings. The Royals' Charlie Leibrandt—perfect through the first five frames—only gave up two hits through the eighth. The Cardinals' Danny Cox allowed hits—seven, in fact—but nothing more, working himself out of a couple of jams, including one in the sixth when he got George Brett to ground into a rally-killing double play.

The Royals' best chance to score came in the seventh, with runners on first and second and Leibrandt at the plate. Prior to the '85 Series, it had been three years since Leibrandt had been to the plate. Needless to say, KC's best move would have been to pinch-hit for Leibrandt and try to manufacture a seventh-inning run, especially in a game where runs were so hard to come by. But manager Dick Howser refused, stuck with Leibrandt (who, admittedly, was pitching masterfully) and watched his overmatched pitcher strike out pitifully on three pitches.

On to the eighth. With two outs and runners on first and second, Cardinals manager Whitey Herzog sent Brian Harper—a little-used utility man—in to bat for *his* pitcher. Harper hit a little blooper to score the all-important first run of the game. "I guess you could say it was my biggest hit ever," Harper said. Quite an understatement, considering it may well have been the hit to win the World Series.

It's important to note here—before we talk about that infamous final inning—that the Cardinals had not blown a ninth-inning lead all season. Todd Worrell, their rookie closer, performed magnificently in his seventeen regular season games, and was even more dominant in the playoffs. In fact, in Game 5, he had struck out *six straight* Royals.

Worrell was righthanded, so as soon as Howser saw him walk to the mound, he went with conventional wisdom and sent lefty Jorge Orta to the plate—a funky matchup to start the ninth.

Here's where things got good.

With two strikes, Orta hit a little nubber off the end of his bat. First baseman Jack Clark charged hard, fielded the ball, and flipped it to a hustling Worrell, who stepped on the bag at just about the same time Orta did.

Now, replays showed that Worrell won the footrace to the bag—just barely. But first-base umpire Don Denkinger called it differently: He signaled Orta safe.

All hell broke loose.

Whitey Herzog flew out of the dugout, shouting and cursing and flailing his rodent-like arms in Denkinger's face. Worrell argued, but he was only a rookie and more than a little out of his element. Clark, angrily wanting to protest, had to be restrained by some of his fellow infielders. Orta stood on first base, ready for the game to continue. And the crowd went nuts, as they sensed the new life that had just been given to their Royals.

It's moments like this, when one team feels gypped, that time seems to drag out. It's almost as if the team doesn't want to return to the contest until their arguments have been heard and the slight corrected.

But Denkinger wasn't about to correct his error. He didn't even want to hear an argument. He was the umpire, he made his call, and no amount of Whitey Herzog arm-flailing tantrum-throwing was going to persuade him to change it.

Fuggedaboudit.

When the game finally resumed, Steve Balboni fouled the first pitch way, way, way up in the air in Clark's direction. Maybe he was still seeing red from the missed call, or maybe he just couldn't see the tiny white sphere in the night sky. Whatever the case, Clark was completely lost. The ball that should have been a sure out dropped near the dugout. And now, by Whitey Herzog's figuring, there should have been two outs. Instead, there were none.

The floodgates of momentum were now open wide.

Balboni chopped a single into the hole between Ozzie Smith and Terry Pendleton. Jim Sundberg, with two strikes on him, laid down a perfect bunt, but Worrell was able to force the lead runner—Orta—at third. Hal McRae came in to hit for shortstop Buddy Biancalana. A noted first-pitch hitter, McRae uncharacteristicly held off, and when St. Louis catcher Darrell Porter allowed a slider to squirt by him for a passed ball, the Cardinals were suddenly looking at runners on second and third, one out, first base open, and another chance to blow a Series-clinching game.

The Cards elected to walk McRae to load the bases and set up a force at any base and a good chance for a game-saving double play.

Dane Iorg—a former Cardinal and 1982 World Series hero (.529 Series average)—walked calmly to the plate. "It's a situation you dream about as a child," Iorg would say later. "Coming to the plate in the bottom of the ninth with the bases loaded and the World Series on the line ..."

Of course, the Cardinals would argue that the World Series should not have been on the line—it should have been over. Orta should have been out at first. Balboni should have been out on the popup. And from there, Worrell would have taken care of business.

But that was hindsight, and what Iorg had was the "here-and-now."

He swung at Worrell's second pitch, made contact—though nothing to brag about—and his broken-bat looper dropped safely in front of Andy Van Slyke in right field. So, okay, maybe it *was* something to brag about, being that it was about to win the World Series.

Balboni walked home for the first run. And there came Sundberg, bar-reling around third, charging for the plate. The throw met him at just about the same time. But Sundberg—a catcher himself who instinctively knew how to avoid a tag on a bang-bang play at the plate—went into a

magnificent head-first hook slide. As he passed the plate—and just before Porter caught up to him—Sundberg reached his left hand out and
brushed home.

The Royals had done it—they'd become the first team all year to come
back on the Cards in the ninth inning.

And the Cardinals—the Nuthouse Gang—were angry. They saw the
replays on tape. They knew they had been hosed out of an out. They believed they had been cheated out of a World Series title. "It's [bleeping]
unbelievable. We're gonna win the [bleeping] World Series and he boots
that play," Herzog said in the visitors' clubhouse at Royals Stadium before hurling a beer bottle into the nearest garbage can.

The Cardinals were deflated. After that, it seemed a formality, really,
that the Royals would be the first team ever to rally in the ninth from the
brink of elimination to win the World Series.

And that's exactly what they did. Game 7 was u-g-l-y. Eleven-to-zip
ugly. Whitey-Herzog-getting-thrown-out-of-the-game ugly. Joaquin-
Andujar-with-veins-popping-out-of-his-head-wanting-to-fight-plate-um-
pire-Denkinger-on-the-mound ugly.

The Cards only alibi for their awful sportsmanship was...well, there
was no good alibi. True, they were like shells of themselves, going through
the motions, with a lack of energy and excitement. True, what had been
the anticipation of celebrating a world championship had turned so shockingly into sour grapes and frustration. But that doesn't translate into
starting fights and calling people foul names.

The Cards knew they'd blown it. They'd blown the 1985 World Series,
after leading three games to one; after needing only to take two of three
at home in front of the sea of red; after watching the plastic being draped
and the victory stand being constructed in their locker room *three games
in a row*.

They didn't want to accept the blame for choking. Whitey Herzog told
the umps during Game 7, "We shouldn't even be out here tonight. You
know you blew that call." Jack Clark, after the loss, said: "These umpires
were over their heads. We got burned on a call that cost us the Series. It's

understandable if we were moody." And Herzog further concluded: "I don't think the Royals could win our division. I don't think they could win the American League East. They struggled in a very weak division."

And maybe the "rodent-at-arms" was right. But the fact is, those struggling Royals beat Herzog's Cards, who *did* win their division.

Sure, maybe it was because The Nuthouse Gang imploded at the worst possible time, but that doesn't strike the word "Royals" from the record books next to the phrase "1985 World Series Champions," and it doesn't replace it with "Cardinals."

27

THE YEAR: 1997
THE VENUE: MGM Grand Garden Arena in Las Vegas
THE EVENT: Mike Tyson vs. Evander Holyfield for the heavyweight championship of the world

OF MIKE TYSON'S first thirty-seven fights, only four *didn't* end with the other guy on the floor—head woozy, knees weak, unable or unwilling to get back up. Tyson fractured jaws, crushed cheekbones, and loosened teeth. He put Marvis Frazier on the mat in thirty seconds. *Thirty seconds.* He unified the three heavyweight crowns, the first fighter to be proclaimed undisputed champion of the world since Leon Spinks. He put the fear of God in every man that met him eye-to-eye on the canvas.

The most intimidating fighter of all time? Probably. A street kid full of rage, Tyson swung his fists like they were jackhammers. Every time Mike Tyson lunged through the ropes into the boxing ring, he only added to his reputation as a punisher, a warrior, a scary sonofabitch. For four years, his stature grew. He became a modern-day Goliath and Scylla and Charibdes and Godzilla and Darth Vader, all rolled into one.

But then his life and career turned into a game of Jenga.

Every time Tyson's boxing prowess took his game to new heights, his personal demons pulled another brick from the foundation he had built.

When his trainer, Kevin Rooney, left after making unflattering public comments about Tyson's marriage to actress Robin Givens, Iron Mike wobbled in the ring for the first time. In his second fight without Rooney, he was knocked out by 42-1 underdog Buster Douglas, losing all three of his titles when he hit the mat.

But...after quickly destroying Henry Tillman, Alex Stewart and Razor Ruddock, it looked like Tyson was back.

Then—as he was set to fight Evander Holyfield for the heavyweight crown—he was convicted of raping a Miss Black America contestant in an Indianapolis hotel room. After serving three of his six-year jail sentence, Tyson was looked at with cautious eyes. And that changed Tyson's intimidation. People weren't fascinated to see Mike Tyson beat somebody to mercy's limit; they were fascinated to see if he would confirm their darkest thoughts right before their eyes on pay-per-view.

By the time Tyson toed it up with Evander Holyfield in 1996, they both held a piece of the heavyweight championship: Tyson the WBC and WBA, Holyfield the IBF. But on that November night, Holyfield showed he wasn't afraid of Tyson, and outboxed him to an eleven-round TKO.

Eight months later, the two warriors agreed to meet again in an incredibly hyped rematch, to be held at the MGM Grand Garden Arena in Las Vegas.

Leading up to it, Tyson promised to be "a lot more intense this time." Holyfield coolly responded: "I don't think there's anything he can do to change the outcome."

Ding-dong.

First-round bell.

Holyfield seemed intent to nullify Tyson's tremendous power by keeping himself as close to Iron Mike as possible. It was a smart strategy, and prevented Tyson from landing any of the big overhand rights that had decimated many a boxer's face. Tyson landed one fist-to-rib blow, but besides that, offered little attack through the first two rounds.

With all the clinching, and very little punching, Tyson was becoming frustrated. He complained about a head butt in the second round, one that had opened up a bloody gash over his eye. But referee Mills Lane shook Tyson off, telling the fighter to get back to it. When the bell sounded to close round two, the crowd started chanting. First, it was, "Ty-son! Ty-son! Ty-son!" But the Holyfield backers interrupted with their own wave: "Ho-ly-field! Ho-ly-field!"

The tension bar rose.

Tyson came out of his corner without his mouthpiece. At the time, it seemed like a mistake, but in lieu of what happened next, it's hard to be so sure. Holyfield pointed out the missing mouthpiece, and Tyson was ushered back to his corner to retrieve it.

With just under a minute left in round three, the fighters were engaged in another clinch, and that's when it happened: Tyson spit out his mouthpiece, rolled his head above Holyfield's shoulder...and bit as hard as he could.

So hard, in fact, that he ended up with a piece of the man's right ear in his mouth, which he also spit out.

Those who paid to view couldn't believe what they had just seen.

Holyfield jumped up and down and spun 360 degrees. The pained, confused expression on his face reflected the same expression that appeared on the face of almost every one of the 16,331 spectators gathered 'round the ring. Referee Lane had the difficult task of trying to sort out this situation on the fly, and Tyson only made matters worse by rushing Holyfield from behind and shoving him. Lane eventually deducted two points from Tyson, and let the round proceed.

Well, of course the fight proceeded furiously, with another clinch...and the most unthinkable thing that could possibly happen happening: Tyson chomped off a chunk of Holyfield's *other* ear.

That was it.

Mills Lane stopped the fight.

And in that moment, Tyson transformed from the mysterious, intimidating, unpredictable R-rated movie hero to the sporting equivalent of the bearded lady—or worse: the masturbating bear at the zoo.

There he was, in the cage that was boxing's biggest ring, in front of all the world to see, acting out without even a thought that anybody was watching him; acting out in a way that was no longer cute or amusing or gripping—it was just pathetic. Over-the-line pathetic. Avert-your-eyes pathetic. Disturbingly pathetic.

It was as if Tyson, who had once been an indomitable warrior, had lost any interest in maintaining his own legacy, his own reputation, his own stature. Actually, it seemed more like he was oblivious to the idea he even held such things.

The once-proud champion had wrecked himself from the inside out.

Immediately, police stormed the ring. But that didn't stop Tyson from trying to rush Holyfield's corner in a fit of rage. "A typical bully move," said Tommy Brooks, Holyfield's assistant trainer. "He'd had him all to himself in the ring, but now, with fifteen people behind him, he suddenly wants to fight. A coward."

The chaos spread from there. As Tyson was escorted out of the arena, two men—who had previously been cheering Tyson—hurled cups at him. Tyson screamed at them and tried to climb the scaffolding after them, but he stopped when he realized they were at least thirty feet away.

Twenty minutes later, Holyfield and all his handlers finally made it back to the dressing room.

A minute or two after that, a ring cleaner named Mitch Libonati knocked on the door.

"I have something Evander probably wants," said Libonati. And he held out the three-quarter-inch-by-one-quarter-inch chunk of skin that used to be the tip of Holyfield's ear. (Oddly enough, the ear tip never made it back onto Holyfield's head. Somewhere between the cooler packed with ice in the ambulance and the hospital emergency room, it was lost. Doctors did the best they could to sew Holyfield up, but plastic surgery would be necessary later.)

Tyson and his handlers eventually ended up in a Range Rover in the parking lot, trying to flee the madness he had created at the MGM Grand. A limo blocked the SUV's path, and Tyson and his guys were stuck in a crowd—not a good situation. A few fans screamed obscenities at Tyson's rolled up windows. One called him a chump.

Bad move, buddy.

Tyson went nuts. He rolled *down* the window and threatened to kill the guy. It looked like he was coming out of the car when, suddenly, the limo backed up and the Range Rover sped away.

The rest of the night at the MGM Grand was filled with unpleasant scenes: A loud bang sent a stampede headed for the door, injuring forty; women fainted; fights broke out.

In the weeks that followed, everybody chimed in, trying to explain, justify, or simply make believable what they had witnessed. Headline writers tried to get their take into just a few words: "Bite of the Century"; "Reality Bites"; "Did Tyson Bite Off More Than He Can Chew?"; "Tyson Bites the Dust, Holyfield"; "Requiem for a Chompion"; "Ear-Responsible"; "Sucker Munch"; and "Pay Per Chew." Boxing haters pointed out that this was the best (worst?) example of what the brutal, combative sport can turn a man into. Boxing defenders suggested Tyson was too dangerous to step into a ring—that his quest to be the champ wasn't pure anymore.

But in the end, none of this was adequate.

How did Mike Tyson stop being Goliath/Scylla/Charibdes/Godzilla/Darth Vader and start being the masturbating bear at the zoo?

Was it an appetite for self-destruction that caused in-the-head Tyson to completely swallow up in-the-ring Tyson?

Is a chewing metaphor the most appropriate thing here? No. But neither is chomping a piece off your competitor's ears when he's beating you. When Mike Tyson did that, he showed the whole world there's a special pathetic-ness in that moment when a bully realizes he's lost his power of intimidation.

28

THE VENUE: The Houston Astrodome
THE EVENT: The "Battle of the Sexes" exhibition match between Bobby Riggs and Billie Jean King

WHILE OUR ENLIGHTENED times call for men and women to be treated equally in the workplace, the term "workplace" doesn't seem to apply to most athletic endeavors. In the sporting realm, it's separate-but-unequal at best (the WNBA and the NBA) and nonexistent at worst.

You'd think that some low-turnout baseball franchise or desperate hockey team would give a woman a shot. Hell, pro baseball even gave 3-foot-7-inch tall Eddie Gaedel (a guy with a one-and-a-half inch strike zone) a pinch-hitting spot during a 1951 St. Louis/Detroit game. (Detroit protested but the Cards had a signed contract.)

Why are the major professional sports the equivalent of the Little Rascal's He-Man Women Haters Club when it comes to admitting women? In the case of football, hockey and basketball, some argue that the physical force demanded by the guidelines of each game will permanently keep the playing field unlevel. That argument is harder to use when it comes to baseball—in fact, minor leaguer Jackie Mitchell struck out no less than Babe Ruth and Lou Gehrig in a serious 1931 exhibition match.

Such rationale is even sillier when it comes to one-on-one, non-contact sports. Why shouldn't a well-trained woman do just as well as a well-trained man in, say, horsehoes? Or chess? Or ski-jumping? Or golf? Or tennis?

Ah, tennis...that rare sport where the women seem to garner as many headlines and as large an audience as their testosteroned equivalents.

Tennis, the perfect, civilized, close-up, friendly, field of battle for a Battle of the Sexes.

The competitors:

Self-proclaimed chauvinist Bobby Riggs, a guy who hit his tennis peak somewhere between 1939—when he won singles, doubles and mixed doubles at Wimbledon, as well as his first U.S. championship—and 1941, when he took his second stateside title. At fifty-five, he was retired from the game. Technically.

Billie Jean King, on the other hand, was twenty-nine and at or near the top of her game. Two years earlier she became the first woman athlete to earn $100,000 in a season (keep in mind, these were 1971 dollars). A three-time winner at Wimbledon, she topped the women's singles rankings five times, sat at the top of the doubles column with Rosie Casals a dozen times, and had just launched the Women's Tennis Association.

Was there ever really a contest here?

Oddsmakers thought so, placing *Riggs* as the favorite.

Why?

Well, it could have something to do with what happened earlier in the year when, having been turned down by King as well as teen star Chris Evert, Riggs found a willing competitor in Aussie phenom Margaret Smith Court. In this round of boy-on-girl action, Riggs started the contest by giving her a bouquet of roses to throw her off, then proceeded to straight-set romp the number-one ranked female in a televised (on Mother's Day, no less) battle. Riggs' statement that "any half-decent male player could defeat even the best female players" now had some evidence—albeit uncomfortable evidence—behind it. He called himself the greatest women's tennis player in the world.

It was kind of embarrassing.

Enter Billie Jean King.

In fact, enter Billie Jean King on a gold litter lifted by a quartet of studly guys, gifting her opponent a baby pig. And enter Bobby Riggs in a rickshaw accompanied by "Bobby's Bosom Buddies" (use your imagination) and offering King a giant Sugar Daddy. Prior to their arrivals, nearly

35,000 spectators—the largest group ever assembled for tennis—entered the Houston Astrodome. And something like 90 million television viewers entered their own living rooms, knowing that this wasn't just a tennis match. This was more akin to a Muhammad Ali title fight, complete with Howard Cosell behind the microphone. This was history.

And this is the part where, in the back of your mind, you start hearing Helen Reddy singing that anthem of feminism, "I am Woman (Hear Me Roar)."

Riggs' rules demanded a best-of-five competition rather than the best-of-three usually played in women's competition. (The Riggs/Court battle was a best-of-three.) King wisely accepted. After all, endurance should give her the advantage. The guy on the north side of fifty—whose training regime included cigars, scotch and vitamins by the handful—should tire out well before set five.

Not that he had that much time to tire out.

King quickly adapted a strategy of hitting softly and making her opponent run as much as possible. It worked. She took the first set, 6-4.

Then she took the second set, 6-3. And Riggs looked every one of his years.

And then she took the third set, 6-3.

Riggs jumped the net to congratulate his better. "Pigs are Dead...Long Live the King" shouted the *Los Angeles Herald-Examiner* headline. The victor's outfit found its way into the Smithsonian's National Museum of American History.

You'd think the world had changed.

And maybe it did, a bit.

Billie Jean King credits that match not only with empowering women in sports and beyond, but also in raising the consciousness of a generation of young men who saw the match. If you were an eight-year-old boy, who would you admire? The gutsy winner or the blowhard loser?

"Most important, perhaps for women everywhere," read *The New York Times*, "she convinced skeptics that a female athlete can survive pressure-filled situations and that men are as susceptible to nerves as women."

Hooray for BJK.

But this book is about losers, not winners. And Bobby Riggs lost more than a tennis match that day. He lost his place in history.

"I'm very proud to have been a part of the biggest tennis spectacular that ever took place," Riggs rationalized to The Tennis Channel, during a special that aired with a rebroadcast of the match in celebration of its thirtieth anniversary. "It was a Bobby Riggs production all the way. Billie Jean was the happiest person in the world, on cloud nine. Women around the world were on cloud nine. They won the dollar bets with their husbands; they won the bets at the office. They forgave me for being a male chauvinist pig after that. I was now the hero."

Maybe.

But there's that little thing called posterity. Just as Bill Clinton will likely be remembered not for his political achievements but for diddling with an intern, Bobby Riggs is remembered not for being one of the greatest players in the history of tennis, but, rather, as the chauvinist who got his ass handed to him.

By a girl.

UNHAPPY ENDINGS

29

THE AXE IS a ten-pound trophy with a fifteen-inch blade that first appeared at a Stanford-Cal baseball game in 1899, when Stanford students used it to chop the head off a straw doll decked out in Cal colors.

Cal students stole it, cut off the handle, and kept it at Berkeley for thirty-one years—until Stanford students stole it back.

Ever since, The Axe has been awarded to the winner of the Big Game. Yes, Big Game—with capitals "B" and "G." We're talking Stanford vs. Cal. The Golden Bears vs. The Cardinal.

The Axe is one of those great college football trophies—like the Old Oaken Bucket or the Little Brown Jug or Paul Bunyan's Axe or the Monon Bell. It changes hands, depending on whether Stanford or Cal wins the year's Big Game.

The Big Game is a big deal, one of the great rivalries in all of sports. So big, in fact, it doesn't seem to need any other adjectives or specificities.

And the eighty-fifth installment of it—in 1982—showcased its most thrilling finish ever.

John Elway, Stanford's senior quarterback, had been groomed for the moment since the day he picked up his first pigskin. Elway was one of the most natural QBs the college game had ever seen. His arm (quick release and incredible velocity), legs (uncanny escapability), veteran leadership and cool-under-pressure demeanor had taken him to greatness: Elway

186

tossed a school-record seventy-seven touchdowns, including six in one game against Oregon State, and, along with Herschel Walker, was a top candidate for the Heisman Trophy in 1982. He led his school, which had won only four games the previous season, to the brink of the Holiday Bowl.

Stanford only had to beat Cal to get there.

And that's what Elway was intent on doing.

He led his offense onto the field with the game on the line. The clock showed 1:27. The scoreboard read: Cal 19, Stanford 17. The ball was marked at the Stanford 21-yard line.

The Cardinal had their work cut out for them.

Elway took a deep breath…and promptly threw two incomplete passes and lost seven yards on a run play, not to mention more than thirty seconds on the clock.

Now…fourth-and-17 from deep in his own territory.

Elway took another deep breath.

Then he completed a long pass for first down. Then another long pass. Big yardage. It was all happening so fast.

Elway pitched back to tailback Mike Dotterer—and caught Cal off guard. Dotterer scrambled for twenty-one yards, finally brought down at the Cal 17-yard line. Twenty-three seconds remained.

Clock started up again. Another running play with Dotterer. Cal was ready for it this time. They dropped the tailback for a short loss. Eight seconds left.

Elway signaled for timeout to stop the clock.

Stanford field goal kicker Mark Harmon ran onto the field. He took his time. Made sure his line was set. Made sure he was set.

Cal play-by-play man Joe Starkey, take it away: "I'll tell you, this is something. For John Elway to pull this out after being fourth-and-17 on his own 13-yard line, with less than a minute to go, is one of the most remarkable finishes you'll ever see.

"Harmon's a great kicker. This is a gimme for Harmon from the 35. A 35-yard kick, eight seconds to go. Mark Harmon. Thirty-five will win it. Listen to the crowd. Here's the snap. Here's the kick. It is long and up…

and it's GOOD! Stanford hits with four seconds to go! And takes a 20-19 lead! Only a miracle could save the Bears as Stanford piles out onto the field."

Oh. So it wasn't a last-second kick. There was still time on the clock. Four seconds, or enough for a miracle, at least. Hmmm.

No matter. It was still the most exciting finish to a Big Game ever. The crowd recognized it. The band recognized it. (They were playing the Stanford fight song "All Right Now" in the corner of the end zone.) The players recognized it more than anybody. White-and-red uniforms swarmed the field to celebrate. Wild, happy mayhem.

Unfortunately, a little too wild. Stanford was assessed a 15-yard penalty on the ensuing kickoff for excessive celebration.

Oh well. It's hard to tell a bunch of college kids not to enjoy the biggest thrill of their lives. Besides, the penalty wouldn't much matter to the outcome of the game. Truth of the matter was, there were only four seconds on the clock: Yes, Cal would be receiving the ball fifteen yards closer to field goal position, but the clock was against them—it was physically impossible to receive the ball, run it into field goal position, and get out of bounds to stop the clock. Which is what Cal would need to do to win the game.

So congratulations John Elway and Stanford. Best finish ever for a Big Game. Barring a miracle, that is, like Joe Starkey said...

• • •

The Play—capital "P"—started out routine. It was a going-through-the-motions kind of thing, just to wipe those four seconds off the clock and put the 1982 Big Game in the record books.

Harmon kicked off, and he squibbed the ball on the ground to make it more difficult to handle. Kevin Moen picked it up and started to run with it. Then he hit a wall of white jerseys.

So Moen turned, planted, and threw an overhand lateral to Richard Rodgers on his left.

Rodgers took the hot potato and ran a few yards with it, then *he* pitched it off to Dwight Garner.

Garner didn't like his own chances, so he quickly gave it back to Rodgers.

Rodgers was in the midst of some serious traffic, and some serious confusion, and right about here is when the Stanford band started walking onto the field, still playing "All Right Now" in celebration. A lot of people—and apparently the band members were firmly in this camp—thought Garner's knee had hit the turf before Rodgers even got the ball, but no whistle had been blown, and there was Rodgers, still running for the end zone.

Rodgers lateraled to Mariet Ford, who broke free from the pack of confusion. He was being chased by a couple of fast Stanford kickoff covermen, and just as they were about to tackle him—at the last possible instant—Ford shoveled the ball, over his shoulder, back to Moen, who'd started the whole nutty thing off.

Now Moen was full speed ahead, and, funny thing, he was suddenly weaving through high hats and drum players and a xylophone guy and the horn section—yes, the Stanford band was marching onto the field.

Moen crossed the goal line untouched—Cal wins! Cal wins!—and as he did, he raised the ball to spike it with two hands. That's when he ran smack into Gary Tyrell, Stanford engineering major and trombonist in the marching band.

Tyrell got absolutely flattened. "I remember looking up at the clock, and I turned to watch all kinds of folks rushing onto the field. I turned around again to find our drum major, and that's when I got plowed over. It looked bad, but it really didn't hurt."

The trombonist ended up on the ground, his dented instrument a few feet away.

And then it ended up in South Bend, Indiana, on display at the College Football Hall of Fame.

Because, in what were supposed to be four let's-just-get-this-thing-over-with seconds, the best finish in a Big Game had become the best finish in college football history...

Moen to Rodgers to Garner to Rodgers to Ford to Moen
And the only thing that stopped them
Was Tyrell on trombone.

189

Of course, when a play as weird as that decides a rivalry as deep as Stanford-Cal, you knew there was going to be controversy.

Now, everyone was on the field: Stanford's players and coaches were out there to argue; Cal's folks were out there to celebrate; and the Cardinal band was out there to…who the hell knows?

But in the middle of it, the refs were conferring. Stanford coaches were screaming that Dwight Garner's knee had been down. To make matters more confusing, one of the officials had thrown a yellow flag, and head official Charles Moffett wanted to make sure his crew made the right ruling.

After the quick conference, the refs unanimously ruled that the penalty was against Stanford—thereby unnecessary to enforce—and that the touchdown counted.

"You would have thought I started World War III," said Moffett, who, ironically enough, was working his last game before retirement. What a way to go out.

There were repercussions of that '82 Big Game. The best was that it put Stanford-Cal right up there with Notre Dame-USC, Michigan-Ohio State, Auburn-Alabama, and Oklahoma-Nebraska as far as great rivalries go. But there were others, too.

Stanford didn't make it into the Hall of Fame Bowl. After The Play transpired, a bowl official found Stanford athletic director Andy Geiger and told him, "Sorry."

John Elway took the loss especially tough. "This is not how I wanted to end my career," he said. And Geiger pointed out: "That game cost John the Heisman Trophy." Herschel Walker got it instead.

When Elway was inducted into the College Football Hall of Fame, he was still talking about The Play: "We just wish we had the band come out for some tackling practice."

The band had its own repercussion, too: They launched a tradition where, every year, the new student band leader officially takes over with four seconds left in the Big Game.

Sadly, Stanford's football program went downhill fast. Its coach, Paul Wiggin, doesn't blame The Play, but allows that it did affect recruiting.

More on point: The Cardinal couldn't get recruits, especially for 1983. "In all honesty," says Wiggin, "I should have walked away at that point. I shouldn't have gone back and tried to pick up the pieces."

But he didn't walk away, and his Cardinal went 1-10 that next season, and Wiggin was fired at the end.

Stanford, however, did manage to get some small revenge. Four days after the '82 Big Game, an "extra" edition of *The Daily Californian*—Berkeley's student newspaper—popped up on the Cal campus. The front page headline: "NCAA Awards Big Game to Stanford." The lead story reported that an NCAA panel had reviewed the controversial kickoff return and ruled Dwight Garner's knee was down before he flipped the ball to Richard Rodgers. Other articles reported quotes from a tearful Coach Joe Kapp and frustrated Golden Bears players.

The whole thing turned out to be a big hoax, produced and distributed by *Stanford Daily* staffers.

But The Play was not a hoax. It was real, it happened, and it was, as announcer Joe Starkey said during his play-by-play, "the most amazing, sensational, dramatic, heart-rending, exciting, thrilling finish in the history of college football."

Suppose that depends which side you take up for.

See, The Axe—one of those great college football trophies that changes hands depending on who wins the yearly rivalry game—is now framed in glass. On it rests a plaque noting the score in each of the 107 versions of The Big Game. Under 1982, it says Cal 25, Stanford 20. Unless Stanford is in possession of The Axe—in which case it reads Stanford 20, Cal 19.

30

THE YEAR: 1984
THE VENUE: San Diego's Jack Murphy Stadium
THE EVENT: Game 5 of the National League Championship Series, Chicago Cubs vs. San Diego Padres

PICTURE A BOOKSHELF. Pretend sports agony is a set of encyclopedias. Now picture its bookends. Can you see them? Bill Buckner on the right and Leon Durham on the left.

Okay, maybe you can't quite picture Durham. Maybe that's because any good sports fan knows Buckner's tragic story, while most folks have forgotten Durham's. Funny thing is, to know one is to know both. Even if you don't know you know both. (Confused? Don't worry. It'll all make sense in the end.)

Leon Durham was nicknamed The Bull. He wore Cubs pinstripes, number ten. Played first base for the most magical Chicago Northsider team in many decades. In fact, the 1984 Cubbies were unarguably the best team in the National League, arguably the best in the majors. (Sure, the Detroit Tigers had a better record, but they beat up on a weak division and played in a league with decidedly weaker pitching.)

The Cubs, though...They had an incredibly well-rounded team whose pitching didn't have a single weak link. On the mound, Steve Trout had thirteen wins and 190 innings pitched. Dennis Eckersley had come over to Chicago from Boston early in the year, and ended up with ten wins and a 3.03 ERA. Scott Sanderson and Rick Reuschel, as spot starters, combined for thirteen wins.

• • •

And then there was Rick Sutcliffe, who also came to the team in a trade early in the year. After arriving in the Windy City from Cleveland, Sutcliffe played on a level almost no one could rise to, going 16-1 with a 2.69 ERA. He completed seven games in twenty starts and was damn near unhittable—which worked out great for the Cubs, because Sutcliffe and the rest of the starters could be counted on to get the ball to 6-foot-7-inch middle reliever Tim Stoddard, who won ten games himself without starting a single one. Then Stoddard handed the ball off to Lee Smith—the nastiest, most intimidating closer in the game in 1984, with thirty-three saves and 86 strikeouts in 101 innings of work.

And as good as the pitching staff was, it didn't have to carry the team, because the offense was better. Ryne Sandberg was an absolute monster; the best second baseman in the league, hands down. He hit for power (nineteen homers and 84 RBIs). He hit for average (.314). He had an astounding nineteen triples. He hit in the clutch, as evidenced by the game in which he whacked two game-tying homers—one in the ninth and one in the eleventh—to spoil the Cardinals' day when Willie McGee hit for the cycle. And don't overlook Ryno's fielding: only six errors in 864 chances. The guy was as rock-solid as they came.

The Cubs whole lineup was rock-solid. Center fielder Bobby Dernier made the offense go: He hit for average, got on base a lot, and swiped forty-five bases on the year. Left fielder Gary Matthews—The Sarge—was the kind of team leader Chicago's Bleacher Bums loved: charismatic, balanced hitter, strong arm. Keith Moreland was a fullback of a right fielder, unafraid to charge the ball or hit with the game on the line. Jody Davis was as productive an offensive catcher as there was, with nineteen homers and ninety-four RBIs. Ron Cey found a home with the Cubs at third base, and clocked a team-leading twenty-five homers and ninety-seven RBIs. Larry Bowa didn't do much hitting, but he was the captain: his very presence in the lineup made everybody play sharper, harder, and with more guts. And The Bull... well, he was the anchor. Hitting cleanup, Durham pounded out twenty-three homers and ninety-six ribbies, hit .279, and committed only seven errors.

What's funny, in an ironic sort of way, was that the Cubs had given up their fan-favorite first baseman in the early-season trade to obtain Eckersley—

a guy named Bill Buckner. It was this move that pressed Leon Durham into duty on the infield. Remember this for later.

The 1984 Chicago Cubs seemed like the team their uber-loyal fans had been waiting for, for years and years and...That season, everything was working out for them. You only need look at the June 23 game, the one where bitter rival the Cardinals and Willie McGee came into Wrigley Field, went up big on the Cubs, had every kind of hit you could imagine (McGee hit for the cycle), and still ended up losing when Sandberg heroically pasted two game-tying homers into the left-field stands off of ace closer Bruce Sutter. The Cubs pulled the rabbit out of the hat in the eleventh inning, sending their fans away from the 12-11 victory with the sense that destiny was finally on their side.

By the end of the regular season, the Cubs racked up ninety-six wins and outdistanced their nearest competition for the division crown—the New York Mets—by 6½ games. The San Diego Padres were up next, in the National League Championship Series. The winner would be going to the place the Cubs had not been since before Ernie Banks played, in 1945—the World Series.

To start the NLCS off right, the Cubs asked the man known as Mr. Cub to throw out the first pitch. As Ernie Banks milled around with the Cubs hitters during batting practice, he pointed out how blue the sky was, how bright the afternoon sun was shining, and most importantly, how stiff the breeze was blowing out to right field. It was a Wrigley regular's dream.

Banks said to the Cubs right fielder, "Keith Moreland, how do you feel?"

Moreland replied, without skipping a beat, "Let's play two," which was Banks' immortal line.

The Cubs were ready. Their magical season was just getting good.

Banks joined in on the magic when he threw out the honorary first pitch. Instead of delivering a straight fastball, he faked catcher Jody Davis—and everyone else in the crowd—with a regular delivery, then flipped the ball forward with his right arm over his left shoulder—a trick he'd learned from Satchel Paige.

The actual between-the-lines Game 1 was surprising and not-so-surprising at the same time. You never expect a team to win in a playoff game, 13-0, when so much is at stake and the pressure is ratcheted up so high. But in that season of Cubs glory, the blowout win at Wrigley seemed to fit right in. Sutcliffe continued his season-long dominance and shut down the Padres hitters, allowing only six hits. Then he watched in awe as his teammates put up two runs in the first inning, three runs in the third, six runs in the fifth, and two more in the sixth. The Cub offense was a machine, thanks in part to the 20 miles-per-hour wind coming out of the southwest. Sutcliffe even got into the act, ripping a towering shot in the third inning that landed out on Sheffield Avenue, past the right-field bleachers. Harry Caray rightfully belted, "Holy cow!" on the pitcher's home run out of the ballpark.

Caray also commented on San Diego losing pitcher Eric Show: "Show spelled backwards is wohs, and that's what he's having today."

Unfortunately for the Padres, Game 2 brought more of the "wohs."

Bobby Dernier got things started for the Cubs right away. He singled to start the Cubs' bottom of the first. Then, when Padre third baseman Luis Salazar fielded Sandberg's grounder and threw to first, Dernier didn't play it safe on the basepaths: He rounded second and slid safely into third. The appreciative crowd gave him a loud ovation. Dernier responded by daringly scoring on a Gary Matthews grounder to short. The Cubs scored three more runs in Game 2, the last on an RBI double by Sandberg. The crowd chanted "MVP! MVP! MVP!" And all the while, Steve Trout held the Padres to two harmless runs, for a 4-2 Chicago victory.

In the best-of-five series, the Cubs had positioned themselves for a sweep. And even if they lost a game in San Diego, the chances of them giving away three straight were...unthinkable. At least the Northside fans thought so; the pennant was in hand.

Game 3 ended up being that one the Cubs could afford to lose. After all, the game was played on San Diego's home turf, with their rowdy crowd juicing up the brown-and-yellow. The Padres were the winners of the National League West, and had earned their way into the postseason. They were a good team that was bound to win one sooner or later. Call it "Later," and mark up a final score of 7-1.

The previous day's victory gave the Padre faithful a certain stir that they carried it with them into the ballpark for Game 4. After each Cub introduction in the pre-game, the crowd would shout in unison, "Who cares?" then cheer wildly at their effort.

In the Padres third, Tony Gwynn brought home a run with a sacrifice fly and Steve Garvey socked an RBI double. Padres 2, Cubs 0. But the Cubs moved ahead in the fourth on a two-run homer by Jody Davis and a solo shot by Bull Durham. Then it became The Steve Garvey Show. The Padres' first sacker tied the score in the fifth with a single. Then he drove in the go-ahead run with another hit. After another run scored on a passed ball, the Padres had a 5-3 lead going into the eighth inning.

Goose Gossage, once an ultra-intimidating closer who was now in the twilight of his career, came into the game to pitch for San Diego. Goose didn't intimidate anyone that night, and promptly gave up a run-scoring single to Moreland and an RBI double to Davis. Tie ball game.

In the ninth, the Cubs handed the ball to their own intimidator—Lee Smith. Smith got the first man out, but gave up a single to hit machine Tony Gwynn. This brought up Garvey. Smith placed a fastball up and out over the plate—a mistake, to be sure—and Garvey laid good wood on it. Jerry Coleman, the Padres broadcaster, called it: "It's gone! The Padres win! Oh, doctor!"

Yes, the Cubs needed a doctor, because their anxiety was suddenly through the roof. They'd blown their safety net, their two-game cushion. And now they faced a one-game test to see who would be traveling to Detroit to play the Tigers in the World Series.

Uh-oh.

The problem with the Cubs was that history was hunting them down. They knew the dates. *1908*: The last time they'd won a World Series. *1945*: The last time they'd even been in a World Series. *1969*: The last time they broke their fans' hearts, losing a comfortable 9½ game lead with six weeks to play, and cementing the term Amazin' Mets in the world's sports vernacular forever.

Now, there was the chance to add "*1984*: The time they had the best team in baseball and blew it as bad as you can possibly blow it."

But the Cubs, in an effort to throw the weight off their shoulders, came out swinging in Game 5. Literally. In the first inning, after Gary Matthews drew a walk, Leon Durham rocked Eric Show's fastball into the seats in right center. In the second, Jody Davis curled a homer of his own around the left-field foul pole, and Rick Sutcliffe—Mr. Unhittable himself—was spotted to a three-run lead. The game, the Series, the Padres season, should have been over.

But in the sixth, the never-say-die Pads rallied. Alan Wiggins laid down a perfect bunt for a hit. Tony Gwynn singled to left. Steve Garvey walked. Bases loaded, no outs. Graig Nettles hit a sacrifice fly to bring home one run. Terry Kennedy hit a line drive to Matthews—The Sarge made the play, but he had to dive for it, and when he did, Gwynn tagged up and scored San Diego's second run.

The game was tight, but the Cubs still led going into the bottom of the seventh.

Not for long.

Sutcliffe walked the leadoff man, Carmelo Martinez, on four pitches— never a good sign of a pitcher's strength. Garry Templeton sacrificed him to second, which brought pinch-hitter Tim Flannery to the plate.

This is where the ball, for Cubs fans, goes into slow motion.

The white orb hops off of Flannery's bat. It squirts toward first baseman Leon Durham. It hits the lip of the grass, right in front of The Bull. It takes a disingenuous hop—lower than Durham had planned for—and scoots under his mitt...between his legs...and out into right field.

Flannery ended up on second base. Martinez ended up crossing the plate. The score ended up tied.

But not for long.

Wiggins dropped a chip-shot single into left field, right in front of Matthews. Flannery held at third. Then Gwynn scorched a liner toward Sandberg. The Cubs second baseman made an attempt at the ball, but, "I played it down, and it went straight up. If I catch the ball, it's a double play, no question about that."

Gwynn's shot went into right-center for a double. Two runs scored. Then Garvey roped one off the mound, bringing home Gwynn.

After four miserable runs, Cub manager Jim Frey finally relieved Sutcliffe. "He had good stuff, he was the best pitcher in the league the last three months, and he wasn't being hit hard," said a defensive Frey. "I thought he'd pitch himself out of the inning."

The rest of Game 5 is un-noteworthy. The Cubs threatened a couple of times—even had the tying run at the plate—but couldn't come back from the dead.

Leon "The Bull" Durham knew: He may not have killed his team, but he had inflicted the first wound.

It's funny how in baseball—most especially in baseball—a play like Durham's error can open the floodgates. Nineteen years later, in the eighth inning of Game 6 of the lengthier NLCS, we witnessed a similar occurrence when a fan named Steve Bartman reached out for a playable foul ball and began the snowball that would ruin the Cubs' best shot at the World Series since, well, 1984.

It's unfair to put all the blame on Durham. In fact, the guy deserves some slack. He had played amazing defense—no hyperbole here: *amazing*—since being forced into first-base duty after Buckner was traded away. In that unnatural position, he'd committed only six errors on the season, for a .994 fielding percentage. Even more incredible: The seventh-inning error in Game 5 of the NLCS was Durham's first non-throwing error of 1984. That's 166 games. So the reality is, The Bull just didn't have very good timing.

Okay, he had awful, horrible, couldn't-possibly-be-any-worse timing.

But, to look at it fairly: The series really shouldn't have gone to a Game 5. Sutcliffe really shouldn't have been left out there after the tying run scored. The Cubs really shouldn't have all the added pressure that eighty-seven years without a World Series title brings.

But that's the way it went.

And that's the way it goes.

And now Durham ends up as a bookend, bronzed, facing Bill Buckner on the other side of the shelf. They're both crouched over, mitts close to the ground (but not close enough), waiting for a ground ball—and a World Series—that just passed through their legs.

31

THE YEAR: 1990
THE VENUE: Louisiana's Super Dome
THE EVENT: The Super Bowl, Denver Broncos vs. San Francisco 49ers

THE NAME John Elway evokes visions of swift feet and unflinching toughness. A cannon arm and a playmaking creativity. A competitor's glare and a winner's smile. Plus, two Lombardi Trophies for winning a pair of Super Bowls.

But what gets buried in the back of our minds, underneath all those rose-colored memories, is this: John Elway and his Denver Broncos lost three Super Bowls in the late '80s and early '90s. No, that should be re-phrased: John Elway and his Denver Broncos were absolutely, thorough-ly, unquestionably *destroyed* in three Super Bowls in the late '80s and early '90s.

1987. Broncos-Giants. Score at halftime: 10-9, Denver. Close game. But, in the third quarter, the Broncs manage just two net yards on ten total plays. They also allow thirty second-half points, a Super Bowl record. Not such a close game. Final score: 39-20, New York.

1988. Broncos-Redskins. Score after one play from scrimmage: 7-0, Denver. Good start. Again. But...in the second quarter, QB Doug Williams and the 'Skins explode for a Super Bowl-record thirty-five unanswered points. Not such a good finish. Score at the end: 42-10, Washington.

1990. The last of the three. The worst of the three.

• • •

By the eve of the AFC Championship Game on January 14, 1990—two weeks before that third Super Bowl—Denver fans weren't sure how to feel.

On the one hand, their team had just put to rest their hated rivals, the Cleveland Browns. Cause for celebration, to be sure. But on the other hand, those two previous Super Bowl whuppings left some Denverites wishing their team had lost to the Browns; it would've saved them the angst.

John Elway took a strong stance against such fans: "Why don't those people go hide in their closets? They're taking the easy way out. If we lose, we lose, but I'd hate to be stuck in a closet."

Elway—like any face-of-the-franchise athlete—had not worked this hard, put in this many hours, or sacrificed this much of his body just to get to the penultimate pedestal. He was a player who shined as brightly as any of the other stars of his day, including Joe Montana, Dan Marino, Lawrence Taylor, Jerry Rice, and Barry Sanders. He took not-so-talented Bronco teams and made them the class of the league—or, at least, the class of the AFC. He performed miracles. And if that's hard to believe, look no further than his 1986 AFC playoff against Cleveland, which can be summed up with two words: The Drive.

Of course, Elway always had a reputation for being The Comeback Kid. In his career, he brought his team from behind with forty-seven game-winning drives. It was not unusual to see Denver fall behind, then courageously dig itself out. And it was their quarterback who always wielded the biggest shovel.

Elway's talents were many—quickness, rifle arm, patient vision, slipperiness in avoiding a would-be tackler's grasp. But those talents were always overshadowed by his grit.

So when his own fans were already picking out the funeral garb for 1990's Super Bowl Sunday, Elway would have liked to refer them to the previous week's Browns game.

The Broncos had taken a big lead in that one, 24-7. But, in a span of four-and-a-half minutes, the Browns scored twice and stood knocking on Denver's—and the Super Bowl's—door, just three points behind. That's when The Comeback Kid morphed into The Stop-the-Bleeding Kid. On third-and-10, in the middle of the field, needing to come away with some points, any points, Elway...rolled right; noticed a ferocious Cleveland all-out rush; spun back to his left; noticed defensive end Bubba Baker set up in his path; also noticed (or maybe it was more like "felt") receiver Vance Johnson as the only Bronco open at the moment, trailing behind the play; still running, threw the ball—without planting his foot—at least 25 yards east-to-west and another 20 north-to-south; and laid the ball directly into Johnson's hands for the back-breaking play of the game.

"You tell me how he does it," Denver's quarterbacks coach, Mike Shanahan, could be heard saying to reporters after the game. "How can he be running left, his toe pointed the wrong way, and still throw it the opposite direction and drop it with perfect touch?"

Grit, we say.

A simple, strong desire to win, Elway'd say.

And the folks looking for the funeral garb would say, "What about '87 and '88? We believed in you then, but ..."

(It was like a chanted argument, going back and forth: "We WON'T get blown out!" "You WILL get blown out!")

Of course, what the fans thought really didn't matter out on the Superdome field. Or in the Denver locker room. What mattered on January 28, 1990, was that the Broncos be able to replace one of their three Lamar Hunt trophies (awarded to the AFC champions) with the Lombardi Trophy. Or, as John Elway liked to put it, "one of those big ones with the football on top."

Their opponent for "one of those big ones with the football on top" was the vaunted, noble San Francisco 49ers, led by uber-winners Joe Montana, Jerry Rice, and Ronnie Lott. These Niners had won three previous Super Bowls. Their offense was poetry in motion, having scored the most points in the league, with two 1,000-yard receivers and a 1,000-yard rusher, not to mention the greatest leader in sports at QB. Their defense was underrated, having held opponents to the third-lowest point total in the league. Which is why, when it came down to it, Denver fans didn't really want to watch their heroes get thrown into the arena with the lions-known-as-Niners.

• • •

Unlike '87 and '88, this one started out bad. *Real* bad. And it got worse from there.

Not that it was John Elway's fault.

In fact, it had nothing to do with his side of the ball, at least not at the start. See, the *Niners* offense had been lying in wait. They'd studied the tapes. They'd prepared a proper game plan. They were just getting impatient for the ambush.

For hints, let's look at the following dialogue, which took place in the weeks prior to the Super Bowl, between San Fran offensive coordinator Mike Holmgren and Joe Montana.

Holmgren: "I hope what I've been watching on film is what we'll see Sunday. What scares me is that it looks too easy."

Montana: "How many of their games have you looked at?"

Holmgren: "Ten."

Montana: "And they've run this defense every time?"

Holmgren nodded.

Montana's eyes lit up: "I can't wait."

Holmgren further clued in the media: "Our guys have all looked at films. They're dying to get out there. Denver plays that old-style 3-4, Cover Three, which is a three-deep zone; or the Cover Two, which is a two-deep. And they don't change. That's the defense that Bill Walsh designed his whole offensive scheme for when he first came to San Francisco."

So, by the time the Denver defense came onto the field, Montana and Co. were growling and howling and roaring. Those cats surveyed the feast in front of them, and from that point on, the devouring could not be stopped.

Five minutes into the game: touchdown.

Fifteen minutes in: touchdown.

Twenty-two minutes: touchdown.

Twenty-nine minutes: touchdown.

By halftime, the 49ers had piled up a 27-3 advantage. And the Broncos were helpless to stop it.

At that point, it became painfully clear: there was no way Elway and his gang could catch up with the cheetah that was the Niner offense. Sure,

Denver had scored a field goal on their first possession, but they looked weird doing it. Within the drive, Elway threw one shovel pass to Bobby Humphrey for 27 yards—a nice gainer. But then he tried it again, and hit Humphrey in the back. When he tried it *again*—When have you ever seen three shovel passes on the same drive except in a high school game involving a team that runs a wicked wishbone?—the ball was almost intercepted by outside linebacker Charles Haley. "This was strange," said 49er linebacker Matt Millen, "like they were setting us up for something that never came."

Thank you for the understatement of the year, Mr. Millen.

And just like the Bronco defense, the offense started bad and only got worse. Which sort of was John Elway's fault.

The Bronco QB wasn't crisp. A couple of his passes were batted away by nickelback Tim McKyer. Ronnie Lott got his hands on another. And once he started pressing for the comeback, Elway threw two interceptions—on the first two possessions of the second half. All told, Elway had his worst game as a pro. He completed ten passes for only 108 yards. His running backs had gained just 64 yards. And he had those two interceptions.

If you're interested, the final score showed: San Francisco 55, Denver 10—the most lopsided Super Bowl in history.

John Elway would go on to win back-to-back Lombardi Trophies. They would be the capstones of one of the three or four greatest quarterback careers of all time. They would also replace two of the three Lamar Hunt trophies in the Denver Broncos locker room.

The long lens of history tells us that all the frustration and downtrodden-ness that came with losing those three late-'80s/early-'90s Super Bowls would be wiped away in, oh, eight years or so.

But you couldn't tell that to the men and women in black, who'd turned off their TVs and started their eulogy right around halftime on January 28, 1990.

THE YEAR: 1991
THE VENUE: Tampa Stadium
THE EVENT: Super Bowl XXV, Buffalo Bills vs. New York Giants

THE KICKER LINED up for the 47-yarder. He took his customary strides backward and did his routine shuffle to the left. In the pause before the snap, he *had* to feel all the heaping tons of pressure that were squeezing down onto his (relatively) not-so-broad shoulders.

See, Scott Norwood had been an NFL kicker for six seasons. Before that, he'd been a USFL kicker for two. Before that, a college kicker at James Madison University. Before that, a high school kicker.

So Scott Norwood knew that the difficulty in the kicker's job was not in the physicality of it. No, that just took a predisposition toward booting an oblong ball and a lot of specialized practice. Plus, a little understanding of physiology. But where the kicker earned his money was in spots like these: The last play of Super Bowl XXV. Eight seconds on the clock. His team down by a single point. The whole football-loving world—and millions of once-a-year fans—watching.

Imagine the pressure.

Scott Norwood could. And it had less to do with the nearly 1 billion people watching the game on TV than with the fact that his kick—make or miss—would conclude The Greatest Super Bowl Ever Played.

It had been that good.

Long before the game actually kicked off, the nation started looking forward to it. Sure, the nation always looks forward to the Super Bowl. But this particular Super Bowl was different. The U.S. was right smack in the middle of the Persian Gulf War with Saddam Hussein's Iraq. America had been occupied with thoughts of war, and the Super Bowl was a welcome distraction, taking folks away from the real world, if only for a night.

So, despite threats of terrorist activities associated with the war—and the knowledge that sharpshooters would be positioned at the upper reaches of Tampa Stadium—almost everybody was hoping for Super Bowl XXV to live up to the game created in their own imaginations.

The Giants and the Bills were two diametrically opposed teams. The Giants were a classic Bill Parcells-coached team: built around the idea that power wins—always. They had a dominating defense, led by their three All-Pro linebackers: Lawrence Taylor, Carl Banks and Pepper Johnson. On offense, Jeff Hostetler was about as gritty a quarterback as you could find, all substance and little style. The offensive line just punished teams. After every game, opposing defenses were left thinking, "Why do we feel so much more beat up than we did last week?" The answer: It was all part of Parcells' scheme. *Run, run, run, throw. Run, run, run, throw. Run, run, run until they're too tired to tackle anymore.*

The Bills, on the other hand, were all style. They were a fluid wave of constant pressure—not physical pressure, but the hurry-up, no-huddle kind. Jim Kelly smoothly and intelligently directed their run-and-shoot attack. He had so many weapons, it was hard to figure out who to stop first. Thurman Thomas could run and catch passes out of the backfield, and he did it so well he gained 1,000 yards each way. James Lofton was stronger and faster than almost anybody who tried to D up on him at his receiver position. His counterpart, Andre Reed, caught almost any ball thrown over the middle, and had a tendency to make the first tackler miss. Add the talented components to the no-huddle system, and you ended up with a "No Stopping Us" kind of offense.

And the Buffalo D was just as impressive. Bruce Smith and Leon Seals rushing the passer, Cornelius Bennett drilling a tight end over the middle, Darryl Talley stripping the ball from the running back behind the line of scrimmage...these are all images that kept Bills' opponents awake at night.

So by the time *these* two teams met up for *this* Super Bowl, the worldwide audience—including soldiers stationed in Saudi Arabia—couldn't wait for them to get it on.

New York scored first, with Matt Bahr hitting a 28-yard field goal after a long time-consuming drive in the first quarter. But Norwood quickly evened things up for quick-strike Buffalo with a 23-yarder of his own.

Then the Bills kicked it into a higher gear, scoring on a 1-yard running touchdown and a surprising safety to grab a 12-3 lead midway through the second quarter. But Hostetler—dropped unkindly by Bruce Smith in the end zone during the safety—bounced back to toss a 14-yard strike to wideout Stephen Baker.

Going into halftime, the Bills led, 12-10. The game was clean (there would be only eleven flags and 66 penalty yards assessed to both teams by the end), and there were highlights on both sides of the ball: punishing tackles, spectacularly slippery runs, and clutch pass-and-catch plays. Both teams played their best when it counted most.

But the Giants—and Bill Parcells' power plan—started to wear down the Bills in the second half. Would-be game MVP Ottis Anderson broke off 3-yard run after 3-yard run. Hostetler calmly converted third-and-longs, the most back-breaking one a 14-yarder to Mark Ingram on third-and-13.

And two fourteen-play, clock-chewing drives later (one of which consumed a Super Bowl-record 9:29), the Bills found themselves in a hole.

A 20-19 hole.

With the game's two-minute warning approaching, those Bills desperately started to claw their way out. First, they finally stopped the Giants downhill-sledding offense, forcing a punt from the Buffalo 48-yard line. Kelly and his Bills offense then took over from their own 10 with 2:16 to go.

Thurman Thomas ripped off a 22-yard run.

Kelly scrambled for eight more.

Tight end Keith McKellar caught a 6-yard pass.

Thomas scrambled for 11 yards to the Giants' 29.

Kelly stopped the clock by throwing the ball down.

And that's where the Bills ended up. Eight seconds remained.

The field-goal unit scrambled onto the field. The play clock was winding down. Adam Lingner grabbed the ball with both hands, ready to snap it on holder Frank Reich's command. Scott Norwood was doing his backstep and slide, and trying to shrug off the pressure...

A 47-yard kick is not a gimme. Not by any stretch of the imagination. A 47-yard kick with the Super Bowl, the long season, some teammates' lifetime dreams—not to mention your own—riding along is not only *not* a gimme; it's the kind of thing that could legitimately implode a guy's brain within his helmet.

Thing is, even if Norwood was able to drown out all those distracting two-ton thoughts, he still had in the back of his mind: *Damn, my guys have just driven back from the dead—they came all the way from the 10-yard line to here, and now, it's up to me to redeem all their blood-and-guts effort. Can't let them down.*

Suddenly, the time was now. *HIKE!* Lingner snapped the ball. Reich got it down cleanly. Norwood made his crescent run and swung his leg...

As soon as he made contact, everyone knew it was wide right. New York fans saw that it was wide, and the prayers of "Please let him miss it" they had been muttering turned into "Please let the damn thing stay out there." Buffalo fans kept wanting—even as the ball was still in the air, turning end over end—the damn thing to draw, to somehow, at the last second, turn inward on a path between the yellow goalposts. But the damn thing never did.

Norwood put his head down, undid his chinstrap, turned and walked away from the Giants diving into piles of jubilation all around him. He kept right on walking through the tunnel, into the Bills' locker room. He—like all the other Bills—was angry, confused, in disbelief.

He sat down in front of his locker. He listened to his coach, kind old Marv Levy, say that he was never more proud of any group of men, and that he could not have asked for anything more from his team. He watched Andre Reed numbly pull off his jersey, and Jim Kelly wipe his soaked face with a towel. He sat still as Levy came to his locker, sat down with him and began to talk.

"I didn't know what to say to him," Levy told *Sports Illustrated*. "I was searching for words to buck him up, but I knew how he felt. We engineered that drive to get him in field-goal range. It was a 47-yard kick off natural grass. Fewer than 50 percent of those are made. He had been such a great kicker for us over the years, and he had won a few games for us with his leg, but you don't think about things like that at a time like that."

So Levy sat there, trying to come up with the appropriate words.

And as he did, one by one, teammates stopped getting dressed and started to come by the locker. Darryl Talley and Nate Odomes were first and second, and they tried to explain that if they had made a tackle on that third-and-13, Norwood would never have needed to make that kick. Andre Reed came over and admitted that if he could have just hung on to a few key passes in the third quarter, the Bills would've won.

Another, then another, then another...Steve Tasker, whose locker was next to Norwood's that Super Bowl night, reinforced it: "None of the players blamed him. They knew you could take back any one play and the game might have been different."

And that was true. But it didn't wipe the slate clean for Scott Norwood.

The great thing about Norwood was, he understood that. He knew he did not come through in the defining moment of his career, the defining moment of his franchise's history, and he was willing to face the anger, the confusion, the disbelief *outside* the locker room—those things that rested with his family, his hometown, the city of Buffalo, the worldwide TV audience, and anybody who would read a newspaper in the next few days.

When the reporters were let into the locker room, *they* started to come by his locker. Well, they didn't so much "come by" as "swarm." Cameras flashed everywhere, incandescent lights shined in Norwood's eyes, and microphones shoved in his face.

Buffalo special teams coach Bruce DeHaven stood next to Norwood as reporters fired their blunt, hurried questions at him.

"How does it feel, Scott?"

"Were you nervous?"

"Did you feel like you hit it good?"

"What do your teammates think?"

"How does it feel to miss that kick and lose the Super Bowl?"

Norwood answered every single one. He stood at his locker for an hour after most of his teammates had left. DeHaven asked him every few minutes, "Do you want me to get rid of these guys?" But Norwood, stand-up guy that he was, said, "I think I owe it to the fans to answer some questions."

Norwood played one more season with the Bills. Then they signed a young stud of a kicker named Steve Christie and waived the thirty-one-year-old Norwood. No other team even called to inquire about his services. He was out of football and underappreciated that fast.

Scott Norwood's story is a sad one about a guy who had his moment, and it could have propelled him to great and everlasting glory in the sports annals, or it could have dragged him to great and everlasting shame.

But, oddly enough, in Norwood's case, neither seems to be the case.

Yes, the guy choked. On the biggest stage imaginable. In the most untimely moment possible. So it should have gone the second way. But his tale doesn't end in bitterness, like Bill Buckner's. It doesn't end in life-threatening tragedy, like Colombian soccer player Andres Escobar's. And it doesn't end in mockery, like Jean van de Velde's.

Maybe it's because his team went on without him to lose the next three Super Bowls and shove his blunder back into the shadows of the number "4" next to the letter "L."

Or, better yet, maybe it's because Scott Norwood, when his painful loss was hiked right in front of his face, and the reporters and city of Buffalo got a good clean hold on it, waiting for the mistake...he didn't run away and sulk, or make any excuses, or ask anybody to feel sorry for him. He took his usual crescent run at it, and swung his leg...

THE YEAR: 1986
THE VENUE: Anaheim Stadium
THE EVENT: Game 5 of the ALCS, Boston Red Sox vs. California Angels

GENE MAUCH HAD managed in Major League Baseball for the better part of twenty-six years, and he understood that there were ups and downs, and winners and losers, and sometimes the sun shined on your ass and sometimes it shined on the other guy's. But for Mauch's entire career, it had been the other guy's. And this caused Mauch plenty of heartache—most poignantly, his 1964 Philadelphia Phillies, who blew a six-and-a-half-game lead with only twelve to go. The guy had come to be known as "The Greatest Manager Who Never Won" because, in all those years, he'd never made it to a World Series.

But 1986 looked different.

For starters, his California Angels team had something he was unaccustomed to: great pitching. Mike Witt was a 6-foot-7-inch fireballer who changed speeds so quickly nobody could keep up. Don Sutton was a magnificent veteran, crafty and solid and unfettered by pressure. John Candelaria was a cool customer with pinpoint control who never let his emotions get the better of him. Kirk McCaskill was a young gun who'd won seventeen games in just his second major-league season. And Donnie Moore was an imposing stopper, the kind both batters and his own catchers feared.

Along with a talented lineup of current and former all-stars—including Brian Downing, rookie Wally Joyner, Doug DeCinces, Bobby Grich, an aging Reggie Jackson, Gary Pettis and Bob Boone—the pitching staff led Mauch's Angels to ninety-two wins and just the third Western Division title in team history.

Better yet, four games into the American League Championship Series, everything was coming up Mauch: The Angels had built a 3-1 advantage over the Boston Red Sox, a lead almost insurmountable throughout sports history. Joy was building in Southern California, and Mauch's players couldn't have been more satisfied to be on the brink of putting their manager into his first World Series.

Up to that point in the ALCS—just as the old saying goes—good pitching was beating good hitting.

In Game 1, Witt thoroughly outpitched the man whom many considered to be his superior—Roger Clemens. While Clemens was giving up four early runs, Witt was clipping along, allowing only five hits in an easy 8-1 California victory.

Game 2 belonged to the Sox and *their* intimidating flame-thrower, Bruce Hurst. He pitched well, but the Angels' terrible play helped, too, in a 9-2 loss. "The last time I saw a game like this," observed Don Sutton, "our coach wouldn't take us to Tastee-Freeze for a milkshake afterward."

Game 3 returned the Angels to form. It was a close one—a pitching duel between Boston's "Oil Can" Boyd and California's John Candaleria— that went into the seventh inning as a 1-1 game. That's when Boyd made two costly mistakes, both with two outs. He hung a slider to Dick "Duckling" Schofield that the Angels shortstop promptly yanked out of the ballpark for a 2-1 lead. Two batters later, he missed his spot with a screwball, and light-hitting Gary Pettis ripped it for a two-run homer. The Angels won, 5-3.

In Game 4, Clemens worked on only three-days' rest for the first time all season. On top of that, he had thrown 143 pitches in his last start (Game 1), so Mauch knew he would be susceptible to a late-game rally. It was just a matter of patience.

In the ninth inning, Boston led 3-0. And if you think about it—three-run lead, Cy Young-winner on the mound, desperation to tie the series— that really should have been enough.

Of course, it wasn't. Because Clemens fell apart. Or, more accurately, he just crapped out.

The Angels took advantage. Schofield and Boone knocked one-out singles. Finally, Clemens was mercifully yanked, and Calvin Schiraldi—Boston's best reliever—entered the game for the save. But the first batter he faced, Pettis, hit a rope to deep left field that Jim Rice misplayed. By the time Rice caught up to the ball, two runs had scored to make it 3-2, Boston.

The Sox intentionally walked California's next hitter to load the bases and ensure a force play at any bag. Schiraldi struck out Bobby Grich with a high heater and he blew two more fastballs past Brian Downing. One more, and the series would have been even at two games apiece. Except Schiraldi didn't throw another fastball. He went with the backdoor slider. And it backed in a little too far—right into Downing's thigh. *Plunk*. The tying run scored on a hit batsman. And two innings later, Grich singled in the winning run. California took its 3-1 series lead.

The Red Sox looked like they would be trampled by the crowded footsteps of their own history—sixty-eight years of chokers and losers and second-place bums.

The Angels looked like they would finally erase the "Greatest Manager Who Never Won" title that went with Mauch's name and replace his memories of second-guessed agony with mound celebrations and clubhouse champagne.

Because a 3-1 series lead was nearly insurmountable.

Nearly.

Game 5 was played in Anaheim. The crowd was juiced, buzzing with pride for its boys, ready to celebrate. And the game—at least until the sixth inning—didn't dissuade them.

Boston jumped on the scoreboard early with a two-run homer by catcher Rich Gedman. Witt was pitching on three-days' rest, and perhaps was a little stiff from the get-go. But once he settled down, he shut down the Red Sox.

Then, in that sixth, trailing 2-1, the Angels' Doug DeCinces hit what appeared to be a routine fly ball. But center fielder David Henderson and right fielder Dwight Evans *both* misplayed the ball, and it dropped between them for a double.

Next up was Grich. He hit a towering fly ball to center, and Henderson jumped at the wall for it, fully extending his arm. He appeared to make a fantastic catch—the kind for which Mel Allen would have said, "How about that!"—and redeem himself for the mis-play with Evans; but the baseball, in fact, hit the heel of his mitt, his glove hit the top of the wall, and the ball caromed over. Home run. Angels lead, 3-2.

Over the next two innings—the seventh and eighth—the Angels scored twice more to build a 5-2 advantage. Going into the final frame, Mauch couldn't help feeling World Series fever. Neither could his players or the fans, for that matter. A homemade banner displayed in the outfield read "ANOTHER BOSTON CHOKE." More accurately, it was about to be "A FIRST ANGELS PENNANT."

And right about here…is where the wheels came off.

Boston's Bill Buckner started the ninth inning with what seemed like a harmless single. Then Don Baylor, with two strikes on him—"I told myself that if this were my last swing, it would be one helluva swing"—put "one helluva swing" on the ball and pulled it over the left-field fence to bring the BoSox to within 5-4.

After Evans made the second out, Boston was down to its last chance to extend the game, Rich Gedman. He had already homered, doubled, singled, and thrown out two baserunners on the day. Mauch was taking no chances with a guy having a career day like that. The Angels' manager brought in left-handed reliever Gary Lucas. Before he even threw one pitch, Gedman called timeout and stepped away from the batters' box. He pointed to the "ANOTHER BOSTON CHOKE" banner, so proudly being displayed in the center-field bleachers. Gedman wanted the sign removed, said it was bothering his vision. After the distraction was taken care of, Lucas threw his first pitch. And…*Plunk*. He hit Gedman.

Yes, he'd taken the bat out of the hot hitter's hands, but he'd also put him on first base.

Well, Mauch was none too happy about that, and wasn't going to take his chances in such an important situation with a pitcher who didn't have good control. So Mauch brought in Donnie Moore, the wickedly intimidating closer.

Now it was David Henderson's turn to be the final Red Sox out.

Only Henderson didn't see it that way. He fouled off a first-pitch fastball. And on Moore's second pitch—an off-speed split-finger that didn't have as much movement as Moore would have liked—Henderson ripped the ball over the left-field fence. Red Sox 6, Angels 5, "ANOTHER BOSTON CHOKE" banner: wrong.

But the game wasn't over. The Angels fought back. They scored a run in the bottom of the ninth. They even had the bases loaded afterward, with Doug DeCinces—a twenty-six-homer, ninety-six-RBI man during the regular season—at the plate with only one out. Almost any decent fly ball, or, obviously, any base hit—would have scored the winning run.

Unfortunately, the Angels' third baseman hit a *shallow* fly ball to right. Then Bobby Grich made the third out, and the game moved into extra innings. "I would have bet my house DeCinces would get that man home," Gene Mauch said in the post-game press conference.

In the tenth, the Red Sox started a rally against Moore. He hit the first batter, Don Baylor, with a pitch. When Baylor trotted down to first base, he stood beside Angel first sacker, Bobby Grich. The two had been close friends for almost twenty years, ever since they had both signed with the Orioles in 1967. "What do you think?" Grich asked Baylor.

"Greatest game I've ever played in," Baylor said.

Grich slapped Baylor five and replied, "Me, too, partner."

And it wasn't even over yet.

Dwight Evans singled off Moore. Gedman, a catcher not known for his speed who—as has been previously pointed out—had been ripping the cover off the ball all day, surprised third baseman DeCinces with a perfectly placed bunt. Bases were loaded. David Henderson was back at the plate. Donnie Moore was in trouble.

Henderson lofted a high fly ball to center. It was just deep enough to get the runner home from third on a tag-up.

That made it 7-6, Sox.

And it brought on Calvin Schiraldi, the goat from Game 4, for a shot at redemption.

Isn't sports great that way?

Schiraldi made the most of the situation, striking out the first two hitters. Then he got Downing to pop up for the final out of the Greatest Game Don Baylor and Bobby Grich Ever Played In.

Of course, it was, at the same time, The Final Heartbreaker for Gene Mauch.

• • •

Who knows what part fate plays in the sporting arena?

Game 5 of the 1986 American League Championship Series gives us much to ponder on the subject.

The Angels turned out to be the chokers, playing the role historically reserved for the Red Sox. Not only did Mauch's bunch give away Game 5, but they went into a corner to sulk and cry for Games 6 and 7—Boston victories by scores of 10-4 and 8-1, respectively. The Angels had, in fact, blown the nearly insurmountable 3-1 series lead.

Boston, on the other hand, by winning and making it to the World Series, set itself up for the greatest disaster in franchise history—maybe the greatest disaster in all of sports' history. Three words can paint the picture: Bill. Buckner's. Legs.

More than one generation of Bostonians would be wounded by that 1986 World Series, and the scarring isn't healing any time soon.

But the saddest consequence of Game 5 involved the Angels' flame-throwing closer. Unfairly blamed for the lost AL Championship Series by the fans and the media, Donnie Moore battled alcoholism and depression for the next three years. Tragically, he took his own life on July 19, 1989.

Gene Mauch, for his part, didn't commit suicide after the Angels blew their shot at glory, but nobody would have blamed him for considering it. To have spent a lifetime investing, working, striving toward the ultimate goal—standing at the top of your profession with the satisfaction of having earned the title "Champion"—to be so agonizingly close...just one strike from the promised land...and to come up short...well, it seems like a special kind of torture.

Gene Mauch retired after the 1987 season. His teams made the playoffs only twice in his twenty-seven years as skipper, and the man never made it to the World Series.

Yet, in the moments following that crushing loss to Boston in Game 5, Mauch showed his true colors as he pondered a return trip to Fenway Park for Games 6 and 7, and how damaging the emotional letdown would be. He kicked his suitcase and said, "I can't believe I have to pack that thing again." Then he added, "And I bet my house that DeCinces would get [the winning run] home. I have no place to sleep tonight."

If only we all had such good humor about our personal debacles.

THE YEAR: 1994
THE VENUE: The Rose Bowl, Pasadena, California
THE EVENT: World Cup soccer match between the United States and Colombia

IN AMERICA, soccer was always a second-class sport. Sure, it was a high-participation sport for recreational youth leagues, but those same kids weren't scrambling for the money and fame of being a pro—at least, not like baseball, basketball or football youngsters did. The best American soccer players didn't even play in America—if they wanted to make a decent-to-exceptional living, they'd have to relocate to places such as England, Germany, and Spain. World Cups past (prior to 1994) further illustrated America's weakness: The country hadn't advanced to the second round since the inaugural event in 1930, and had gone forty-four years—since 1950—without a single victory.

Colombia was an altogether different story. In Colombia, a soccer field was and is the only place in which the country can compete on a world stage. It's *the* sport. Even on a continent wild about soccer, Colombia always separated itself from the pack with rabid fans and unbelievably high expectations.

Loaded with talent, the 1994 team was peppered with fluid, fast, intelligent athletes, who played with purpose and execution. They were explosive. They were skilled. They were used to the pressure of playing on the world's biggest sporting stage. They were the popular world choice to win the whole damn thing. Their countrymen knew it, and expected greatness. Even more greatness than usual.

One of those countrymen, on the eve of the World Cup match between Columbia and the United States, faxed his beloved team's hotel in Fullerton, California, stating the harm that would come to Colombian coach Francisco Maturana, midfielder Gabriel Gomez, their homes and their families if the team were to lose.

It was a threat easy to dismiss, given the history of poor United States showings in World Cups coupled with Colombia's talent pool. In fact, as soon as the matchups were announced—months before the June 22 game with the U.S.—Colombian sports commentators were promising victory. This would be more than a game. Colombians knew that the name of their country brought to mind the late cocaine kingpin Pablo Escobar, and everything he represented. They also knew that this was their chance to erase that image. And to replace it with one of excellence and victory.

Out on the Rose Bowl grass, 93,000 spectators were watching another Escobar play defense as the Americans went on the attack. Growing into an international star himself, Colombia's Andres Escobar was fast and fluid, with seamless footwork, outstanding leg strength, and a world-class ability to throw himself into the thick of things to break up a scoring possibility. Escobar was gaining a reputation as one of the best defenders in the soccer world, and was certainly at the peak of his prowess during the 1994 World Cup.

But here came U.S. midfielder John Harkes, charging down the left side, pushing the ball in front of him. Knowing he did not have a clear shot on goal, he instead offered a crossing pass to a teammate on his right.

The teammate never received the pass.

Andres Escobar, using all the quickness and determination he could muster, desperately lunged for the ball. He had to switch directions. He had to stick his leg backward. He had to clear that ball. He had to…

But the worst thing happened: Rather than cruise into safe territory, the ball went spraying toward the Colombian net. Goalkeeper Oscar Cordoba couldn't react quickly enough. He tumbled backward and lay on the ground, stunned.

In soccer parlance, what Andres Escobar did is known as an "own goal."

It's humiliating enough in a regular-season game.

This was the World Cup.

That "own goal" not only impacted Escobar's game, it also seemed to crush the spirits of his teammates. Not even star scorer Faustino Asprilla could connect ball to net.

In the second half, forward Ernie Stewart scored the game-clinching goal, putting the Americans up, 2-0, and rendering irrelevant a Colombian last-ditch-effort goal in the game's final minute. The U.S. moved into the second round, and Escobar, Asprilla, and company returned home to shattered dreams.

In the aftermath, a gang of angry gamblers pointed a gun at Asprilla's wife and drove away with her Mercedes, calling it a "down payment on what you owe us." He soon relocated to Italy. Coach Maturana resigned.

But nobody felt the pain of the loss like Andres Escobar, who became the national goat. He also proved a blessing to an American media who needed just that kick of luck to churn up the soccer machine in their own country. *Sports Illustrated* even wrote, "For all the American obsession with…Pablo Escobar, this was an ironic turn of events: Escobar's dead; long live Escobar!"

Unfortunately, that *Sports Illustrated* quote was the beginning of an even graver ironic turn.

On Friday, July 2—only ten days after the loss to the United States—Escobar was back in Colombia, sympathetic to the pain and anger of his countrymen, and privately more distraught by his own misplay than anyone. But publicly, he had decided that a resilient, prideful face was the one to put on, signaling that he was moving forward and carrying on with his life.

So Escobar did what he often did on Friday nights—dancing and talking until the wee hours of the morning with friends at the El Idio nightclub on the outskirts of Medellin.

At about 3:30 a.m., Escobar left El Indio. That's when he was accosted by three men and a woman. They insulted him. He shouted back.

Suddenly, a gun appeared.

Suddenly, one of the hecklers shouted, "Thanks for the own-goal, hijueputa!" (Translation: "son of a whore.")

And suddenly, Escobar was on the ground, groaning and clutching a chest shattered by six bullets.

An immediate trip to the hospital was of no use: the soccer star was pronounced dead on arrival.

In the months that followed, a man named Humberto Munoz confessed to the murder and—surprising in a country where more than 98 percent of the 30,000 annual homicides go unpunished—actually served jail time. All charges against the other two men arrested—Pedro Gallon Henao and Juan Gallon Henao—were dropped for lack of evidence.

Can we chalk Andres Escobar's life up to being the cost of a lost soccer game?

Well, yes and no. True, Escobar scored a decisive goal for an opponent in the most important loss he would ever play in. But he also cost a lot of powerful, short-tempered people a great deal of money. Noted Andres' father, Juan Jose Escobar: "The sport is so infiltrated with bad guys that any attempt to rip out the mob is automatically thwarted by institutionalized corruption and inertia."

Sounds like Dad's talking about the real losers in this tragic story that basically boils down to a guy who was in the wrong place at the wrong time, trying to do the right thing.

And now Andres Escobar has been forever robbed of the one good thing about losing: redemption.

35

LET'S PRETEND.

Okay?

Good.

Pretend you don't remember the twenty-two seasons spanning *four* decades.

Or the .289 career average.

Or the 2,715 career hits—more than all but fifty guys who've ever swung a bat.

Pretend there were no good moments in his career.

Pretend there were no *other* moments in his career.

No All-Star Game in 1981.

No 1974 NLCS Championship.

No '86 ALCS Championship.

No 1980 National League batting title.

No record-setting 184 defensive assists as a first baseman in '85.

No all-guts inside-the-park-homer at Fenway in his last season in the majors (1990).

No all-important rally-starting single to start the ninth inning of one of the most exciting ALCS games ever—Game 5 versus the California Angels.

No burned-into-the-memory bear hug with David (Hendu) Henderson after Hendu's Series-saving homer in the same inning.

Pretend you didn't notice Billy Buck's hightops in that '86 World Series.

Pretend you didn't know he wore those hightops to provide support for his always-painful, all-but-eroded ankles, which most guys would have quit playing on years ago.

Pretend John McNamara—Buckner's manager in '86—*should* have let him stay out there during that tenth inning of Game 6 against the Mets, with a two-run lead and Billy Buck struggling at the plate, knowing the first baseman moved like a creaky old man with a walker because of those bum ankles *and* that defensive whiz Dave Stapleton—who McNamara usually subbed for Buckner—was still available on the bench.

Pretend nothing happened before Mookie Wilson came to the plate.

Hendu didn't homer in the top of the tenth to give the Sox a one-run lead.

Wade Boggs didn't double home Dwight Evans for an insurance run.

Calvin Schiraldi didn't come in to pitch the bottom of the inning, and he didn't quickly strike out Mets Wally Backman and Keith Hernandez.

Gary Carter didn't rip a single.

Kevin Mitchell didn't also rip a single.

Nobody watching the game on TV saw the most portentous live footage ever spliced together (which NBC should've won an award for): Roger Clemens sitting on his hands in the dugout; Schiraldi wetting himself on the mound; Bob Stanley frantically loosening up in the Sox bullpen. Further, nobody could sense the impending doom.

Ray Knight didn't wait to get two strikes on him, *then* fist a little blooper just behind second base that fell for a base hit.

Carter didn't score. And Mitchell didn't move over to third, either.

Bob Stanley—Boston's inconsistent reliever—didn't jog in from the bullpen.

Mookie never stepped up to the plate.

Mookie didn't get two strikes on him, the second one an agonizing roller down the third base line that, if it stayed fair, would have been Out Number Three.

Bob Stanley didn't try to come inside on Mookie. And he didn't almost hit Mookie in the feet. That pitch wasn't wild, and it didn't get past Rich Gedman, allowing Kevin Mitchell to score the tying run.

Now, go ahead, pretend Mookie never hit that slow roller, bounding toward Billy Buck—in his hightops and mustache and moving like a fifty-and-over slow-pitch softball player who hasn't stretched yet—like an ever-increasing-in-size cartoon bowling ball.

Pretend that if he would've fielded the ball, Buckner would've been able to beat speed-demon Mookie to the bag.

Pretend that the Mets wouldn't have won Game 6, anyway.

Pretend nothing happened *after* that ball went through his legs.

Pretend that there was no rainout that gave the Sox a day to mentally recover from Game 6.

Pretend the Sox had any chance at all to win that Series after such a disastrous crash-and-burn—many would argue the most disastrous of all time.

Pretend the Sox didn't also blow Game 7, when, after leading 3-0 through five innings, they ended up on the wrong side of the 8-5 score.

Pretend the Mets weren't the World Champs when the Red Sox should have been.

Pretend, if you're the kind of person who talks to your buddies or your mom or dad or your brother or sister about sports, that you've *never* called Bill Buckner a loser, a goat, a bum, a chump.

Pretend it's "justice" that Buckner will never be remembered for what a great player he was in his career, but only for that one ground ball that went through his legs.

Pretend Buckner's infamous moment is the result of not enough practice, or a brain fart, or the worst—just not giving a damn.

Pretend we shouldn't sit here and ask you: Why is it only Buckner that gets the blame? What about Gedman and Stanley and Schiraldi?

Pretend Bill Buckner doesn't feel alone and ostracized, and that he likes keeping to himself in Idaho.

Pretend there are no other guys out there, on diamonds or courts or fields all across the country—in this decade or the last decade or the one before or the one before that—who've committed the error, made the mistake, bumbled the game.

Pretend you never heard of Game 6.

Pretend the ball didn't go through his legs.

Pretend Bill Buckner doesn't exist.

Just don't pretend you never felt sorry for him.

APPENDIX A

ALL THE FIELD'S A STAGE

VERY RARELY does history tell of a plumber who was so successful at plumbing that he thought he could perform brain surgery. Nor do we hear of expert seamstresses who, on a whim, take it upon themselves to fly airplanes.

Yet…rarely does a season go by that some world-class athlete doesn't decide to take on some high-profile acting, singing or other entertainment biz gig. This is usually done under the belief that, for example, the same skill set that helps drive a baseball over a center-field wall can be used to create, say, a satisfying rap album.

Of course, there are crossover successes. Johnny Weissmuller. Jim Brown. Bubba Smith. And, yes, Norwegian skater/1940s Hollywood starlet Sonja Henie. What did these folks have in common? They knew their limitations. Let us repeat: They knew their limitations.

Not all athletes get that.

Which is why we opted for two lists. First, the soured cream of the crop who tried to make a splash in front of the cameras.

Next, you'll find a sad list of those who somehow believed that there was a place for them in the recording studio.

And so we offer Moonlighter's Madness (Sports Edition)—our tribute to the most embarrasing performances by an athlete…

10. Shaquille O'Neal in *Kazaam*

Shaq stars as a three-wish-offering, boombox-trapped genie and gives a performance that would be booed off a community theater stage. And he can't blame anyone else for this mess, since he also served as executive producer.

9. Carol Heiss in *Snow White and the Three Stooges*

She was a five-time world champion figure skater. She won a silver medal at the 1956 Olympic games and a gold four years later. How does

Hollywood welcome her? By casting her in the first of the title roles in a past-their-prime *Three Stooges* vehicle. Larry shows more range.

8. Mitch Gaylord in *American Anthem*/Kurt Thomas in *Gymkata* (tie)

Two gymnasts try to bounce off the trampoline of sports success and try to clutch the high bar of Hollywood stardom. Gaylord sticks pretty close to home—a guy trains for the Olympics. Thomas tries to save the world. Both earn permanent spots on the double feature at the Hell's Gymnasium/Cineplex.

7. Kareem Abdul-Jabbar in the "Giant" episode of *Man from Atlantis*

Okay, we'll give him points for his funny performance in *Airplane!*, but that doesn't erase the traumatic memory of the basketball star's performance as Thark—yes, Thark—a mysterious nine-foot-tall creature causing trouble for our undersea hero.

6. Wilt Chamberlain in *Conan the Destroyer*

Shazaam. Thark. Now Bombaata. Note a pattern forming here? Future wannabee actors make note: DON'T PLAY A CHARACTER WITH A STUPID NAME. Even if you get to hang out with Grace Jones and the future governor of California.

5. Roosevelt Greer in *The Thing With Two Heads*

Ray Milland plays a racist who—surprise—finds his head grafted onto the shoulder of death row inmate Rosie Greer. Fledgling actors are told to try to work *with* the best actors in the business, not share roles with them. The results are terrifying, but not in the way the filmmakers intended.

4. Hulk Hogan in *Mr. Nanny*

The Hulkster makes *Who's the Boss?*-man Tony Danza look like Laurence Olivier.

3. Bruce Jenner in *Can't Stop the Music*

Six flamboyant singers. A director (Nancy Walker) best known for performing in paper towel commercials. Steve Guttenberg in the lead. Sounds perfect...only we're missing something. What could it be? Thinking. Thinking. That's it! We need a world-class Olympic athlete. Now it can't fail.

2. Earvin "Magic" Johnson on *The Magic Hour*

For a few weeks back in 1998, Magic's talk show was the single most excruciating hour on the tube...night after night after night.

1. Evel Knievel in *Viva Knievel!*

What makes this performance rise above (or, to be more accurate, sink below) the others on this list? Not that Knievel surrounds himself with such noted actors as Gene Kelly, Lauren Hutton, Leslie Nielson and Dabney Coleman. Not because it is implied that hanging around the cycle jumper can make lame kids walk (seriously). Not because Evel foils drug dealers. No, the reason we're giving him the honor of Worst Performance by an Athlete in a Starring Role is because, in *Viva Knievel*, Evel Knievel sucks *at playing himself!*

APPENDIX B
CONCRETE VOICES

"DON'T WORRY that it's not good enough for anyone else to sing," sang an ancient sage who, we believe, was a carpenter. "Just sing. Sing a song."

Well, maybe that's not always such great advice. Particularly in the case of these athletes who inflicted their musicianship upon a world that, really, should know better.

5. Terry Bradshaw: *Terry and Jake*

The legendary quarterback lopsidedly joins forces with Grammy-winning gospel artist Jack Hess (who, in better days, recorded with Elvis Presley). Save us.

4. Carl Lewis and the Electric Storm: *Break It Up*

This single, which sold 25,000 copies in the U.S. and 500,000 in Europe, isn't nearly as bad as Lewis' infamous national anthem. Then again, neither is Bruce Willis' "Respect Yourself."

3. Shaqille O'Neal: *Shaq Diesel*

This album—which includes such tunes as "I Hate 2Brag" and the inevitable "Shoot Pass Slam"—is to rap music what…well, what *Kazaam!* is to cinema.

2. Oscar De La Hoya: *Oscar De La Hoya*

The world champion boxer covers, among other songs, the Bee Gees' "Run to Me" and comes across as a teen abandoned by the rest of his boy band. At least there's not a song called "Punch Duck Punch."

1. Macho Man Randy Savage: *Be a Man*

Pro wrestling may not be real—but the pain inflected on the ears of listeners is beyond question quite authentic. Still, you've got to admire a (macho) man who can rhyme "up" with "butt."

APPENDIX C

LEAGUES OF THEIR OWN UNDOING

IT'S ONE THING to achieve your personal worst or to be responsible for blowing your team's dreams. It's disaster writ on a much larger scale when an *entire league* goes bad, a season is blown, or a chunk of games are missed—because of arrogance, stupidity, taking things for granted, or all of the above. You'll see...

THE LEAGUE: MLB

WHAT HAPPENED: Owners saw the need for revenue-sharing—small-market teams getting help from big-market moneymakers—but also believed a salary cap was needed to offset the revenue-sharing. Players didn't like the idea of having to solve the owners' financial disparities. So, making the case that money truly is the root of all evil, Major League Baseball players went on strike on August 12, 1994—just as their fans were starting to catch pennant fever for the World Series right around the corner. Bad, bad, bad move. MLB lost the rest of the 1994 regular season and, more importantly, the playoffs and the championship series. To this day, some fans refuse to return to "the national pastime."

TO SUM IT ALL UP... Phillies center fielder Lenny Dykstra: "For the first time in my career, I really felt like we were [bleeping] the fans. Without them, there's no big salaries, no Porsches."

THE LEAGUE: NBA

WHAT HAPPENED: In 1998, the NBA Players Association and the league's owners had their own labor dispute over, among many tedious details, including maximum salary, agents' power, and the length of term before a player becomes an unrestricted free agent. In other words, what was publicly called a "collective bargaining agreement" was really just rich guys squabbling with richer guys over loads of money. Fans missed thirty-two games and three months of NBA basketball, and, all told, the owners' lockout lasted 191 days. Luckily, though, the NBA Playoffs and Finals remained intact.

TO SUM IT ALL UP...players union president Patrick Ewing, of the New York Knicks, who tried to rationalize his side thusly: "We might make a lot of money, but we also spend a lot of money."

THE LEAGUE: CBA

WHAT HAPPENED: In 1999, NBA great Isiah Thomas bought the then-53-year-old Continental Basketball Association for $9 million, paying $4.5 million up front and promising to pay the rest over four years. Eighteen months later, and a month into the 2000-'01 season, the CBA had lost more than $1 million and was struggling to make payroll. And its "champion," Thomas, put his ownership in a blind trust while coaching the NBA's Indiana Pacers. By the time the CBA officially filed for Chapter 7 bankruptcy, the league submitted 744 pages of unpaid bills totaling $4.7 million, and 101 pages of overdue wages. It listed its only assets as: old uniforms, twelve cars, office equipment and the value of its team logos.

TO SUM IT ALL UP...former Fort Wayne Fury owner Jay Leonard, who said of Isiah Thomas: "It is like he bought a car on a five-year loan, drove it for two years, blew the engine, dropped the trannie and then drove it back and said, 'Here, you can have it back.'"

THE LEAGUE: XFL

WHAT HAPPENED: For some reason, America just didn't embrace the idea of a football game in desperate need of Ritalin. This made-for-TV league, created and developed by wrestling mogul Vince McMahon, debuted on Saturday, February 3, 2001, in primetime on NBC. It prominently featured game footage from cameramen standing on the field during live action, cheerleaders wearing next-to-nothing, Jesse "The Body" Ventura as color commentator and a guy sporting "He Hate Me" on the back of his jersey. That first weekend, the league netted huge ratings television ratings and sold out stadiums in Las Vegas and Orlando. But by week number two, the ratings fell off a figurative cliff. Three months later, the

Xtreme Football League was garnering the lowest prime-time ratings in the history of network television. Apparently, it is possible to underestimate the intelligence of the public.

TO SUM IT ALL UP...*Los Angeles Times* sports editor Bill Dwyre, when asked if his paper had a beat writer covering the hometown Los Angeles Xtreme: "Oh, good God, no! Please!"

Books of Interest

New York Times Bestseller!

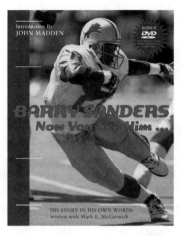

Barry Sanders
Now You See Him...
His Story in His Own Words
By Barry Sanders with Mark E. McCormick

The fans have spoken, catapulting Barry Sanders back on top of the game. Barry's lifetime achievements on the gridiron culminated in his election to both the Pro Football Hall of Fame and the College Football Hall of Fame in 2004.

In this *New York Times* bestseller, Barry breaks his silence for the first time ever and reveals why, as one of the game's most exciting and explosive running backs, he abruptly retired just as he was closing in on the all-time NFL record for most yards gained. The book also captures the high points of his athletic career, complete with original commentary from Emmitt Smith, Lomas Brown, Mike Singletary, and others.

Barry Sanders: Now You See Him... also includes a specially produced DVD showing one of football's greatest players in action. A rare treat for any football fan.

Price $29.99 Hardcover
ISBN: 1-57860-139-8

To order call: 1(800) 343-4499 www.emmisbooks.com
Emmis Books 1700 Madison Road Cincinnati, Ohio 45206

Books of Interest

Baseball Behind the Seams

The **Baseball Behind the Seams** series by Rob Trucks presents baseball the way it ought to be: no pouting superstars, no steroids, no players' strikes. Each of the books in this one-of-a-kind series focuses on a single position, exploring it with the kind of depth serious fans crave. Through extensive research, including interviews with more than a hundred players past and present, Trucks has brought together the most original and informative series ever published on the game.

Each book in the series covers
- The physical and mental qualities of the position
- The position's history
- The plays, and how to make them
- Profiles of the position's top all-time players
- The best defenders of the position
- A day in the life of one player, from arriving at the ballpark to the final out
- Lists of Gold Glovers, MVPs, and Rookies of the Year
- Fun and quirky facts about the position

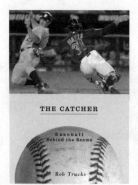

The Catcher
By Rob Trucks

The Catcher is an in-depth exploration into the most demanding position in baseball. Two-time Gold Glover Charles Johnson of the Colorado Rockies, one of the few African-American catchers in major-league baseball, takes the reader

Books of Interest

through a game behind the plate. *The Catcher* brims with photos and illustrations, along with profiles of such great catchers as Johnny Bench, Yogi Berra, Bill Dickey, Gary Carter, Mickey Cochrane, and many more.

Price $14.99 Paperback
ISBN: 1-57860-164-9

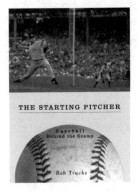

The Starting Pitcher
By Rob Trucks

No position on the field receives more attention from fans as the starting pitcher, and yet this is one of the most misunderstood positions in all of baseball. To put the reader behind the seams and into the mind of the man on the mound, Rob Trucks has conducted dozens of in-depth interviews with players, coaches, and scouts to provide a true insider's look at this key position. The "Day in the Life" chapter features Andy Pettitte.

Price $14.99 Paperback
ISBN: 1-57860-163-0

To order call: 1(800) 343-4499 www.emmisbooks.com
Emmis Books 1700 Madison Road Cincinnati, Ohio 45206

Books of Interest

Thursday's Game
Notes from a Golfer with Far to Go
By Tom Chiarella

Tee up with Tom Chiarella, golf columnist for *Esquire* magazine and contributor to *Links* and *Washington Golf Monthly*. With the keen eye of a regular guy, Tom plays courses that most duffers can only dream of—leaving divots, lost balls, and the occasional picture-perfect pin shot in his wake. Tom brings his A-game, complete with a wry sense of humor and a quick "Fore!" whether he's playing in Scotland, Morocco, Pebble Beach, or his favorite par-three in Terre Haute, Indiana.

Join Tom as he spends a few days with roguish pro John Daly, plays a round with actor Billy Crudup, and hits the links with Vegas singer Don Cherry. Regardless of where he is or who he's playing with, Tom keeps his wit in the fairway and his shots in the rough, making for a wonderful armchair companion.

Golfers everywhere will identify with Tom's tales of low-grade frustration centered on a dimpled ball and a fairway filled with traps. But these affectionate, tee-in-cheek reminiscences and respectful rantings are balanced by memories of those sublime—and all too seldom—moments when the shot rises like a rocket, straight and true, carrying over a long stretch of treacherous real estate to settle at last onto the cool comfort of the green.

Price $22.99 Hardcover
ISBN: 1-57860-170-3

To order call: 1(800) 343-4499 www.emmisbooks.com
Emmis Books 1700 Madison Road Cincinnati, Ohio 45206